My Kind of Town

My Kind Of Town

An Essential Guide
to Finding the
Ideal Place to Live

by Eric and Margaret Burnette

CHRONICLE BOOKS
SAN FRANCISCO

Library of Congress Cataloging-
in-Publication Data available.

ISBN 0-8118-0764-9

Note to Readers
If you have any stories,
observations, information,
emerging trends, or suggestions to share with the
authors, please contact them
care of Chronicle Books or
through their Internet address:
KindofTown@aol.com

Printed in the United States.

Cover design: Jon Hersey
Book design & Composition:
    Mark Jones

Distributed in Canada by
Raincoast Books
8680 Cambie Street
Vancouver, B.C. V6P 6M9

10 9 8 7 6 5 4 3 2 1

Chronicle Books
275 Fifth Street
San Francisco, CA 94103

"This City Isn't Home, We Just Live Here"

We were driving our friends nuts. They couldn't believe that we wanted to leave the San Francisco area. To them it was like wanting to leave paradise. But with each passing year we felt less at home there.

We both grew up there. Our families live there. Old friends are there. The climate is great. It is a cultural beehive. It is a place of incredible natural beauty. Margaret had a great video production job with a major computer company. Eric worked as a merchant ship officer on ships that often came in and out of San Francisco Bay. Yet we were slowly coming to the conclusion that we no longer belonged where we had both grown up. The idea of moving kept creeping into our conversations.

There were concrete factors we could point to: Manhattan prices without Manhattan delicatessens. Increased rates of violent crime. Freeways that functioned like endless parking lots. Grumpy yuppies flunking their stress-reduction classes. Absurd prices for housing. There were also personal reasons for wanting to leave the San Francisco area: Too much emphasis on earning and too little on living. The financial pressures of high housing costs. The time pressures of two demanding careers. Too little time for family and friends. Too many worries about the welfare and education of our young son. All these factors added up to a feeling of alienation. It was just a place to live. It didn't feel like home anymore.

As the months rolled by our resolve hardened. We intended to move. If only we could figure out where. We didn't want to move just for the sake of stirring change into our lives; our quest was for a place that felt like a hometown. We wanted to find some corner of the United States where it was possible to enjoy a more balanced, fulfilling style of life.

We quickly ruled out moving to another metropolitan area. Why trade one set of aggravations for another? At least we had friends, family, and good jobs in the San Francisco area. Moving to a remote farm area didn't seem like such a good idea either. It just wasn't our style. Raising pigs and cows is a noble livelihood, but it's not for us.

There is a time for departure even when there's no certain place to go.

—Tennessee Williams
Camino Real

"Best Places to Live" for Whom?

Our search for a new town was haphazard at first. We randomly asked people about regions, towns, climates, local economies, and a thousand other things. We hoped to stumble across some place—anyplace—that was right for us. We began to scour bookstores and libraries for information that would direct us to the small cities and towns best suited to our needs. We found books about job opportunities in different areas, about the quality of life in various cities, about the recreational facilities in different states, about organizing your relocation, and even about moving your pets. Nowhere could we find resources to help us answer the most crucial question of all: Where is the best place for *us* to live?

Articles listing "The Best Places to Live" were everywhere. But the best places for whom? They generally listed larger cities. We were familiar with cities at the top of those lists and considered several suitable for tire recapping operations, hazardous waste disposal sites, or rendering plants. While they might have been good for somebody else, they were dead wrong for us. What did that say about all the rest of the cities on those lists? As far as we were concerned, they all had to be suspect.

We realized that in order to find the type of town we sought, we needed to create our own personal "best places" list. With a list that was based on standards we created, we would find a place that fit *our* unique, individual needs.

Individual Needs

Do not think for a minute that both of us wanted the same things in a place to live. We did not. Margaret loves going to museums, plays, concerts, foreign films, and art bars. Eric is happy spending an afternoon hanging out at a small airport or fishing wharf. Margaret's profession as a writer/producer requires that she live near a city of at least medium size. Eric's career as a merchant ship officer would allow him to live on the side of a mountain in Nepal during periods not at sea. Video production depends on networking. Being a ship's officer doesn't. Margaret is social. Eric is a loner. These contrasts run unbroken throughout our lives.

From this description of ourselves, it would seem that no city or town on earth could satisfy either of us without one of us making a massive compromise. But in fact, we have found a place that is mutually satisfying. True, the choice involved some compromise for each of us. But the compromises were small compared to the overall improvement in the quality of both of our lives. We each gave a little and we both gained a lot.

Children

We had one child at the time we seriously started to consider moving to a smaller community. Douglas was about five, and soon to start elementary school. It was clear that, even though we lived in a city with one of the best school districts in the nation, Douglas was still going to be in a large classroom, in a large school, in a large school system, with shrinking funds and growing teacher dissatisfaction. He would get very little individual attention. Our "top" school district was looking like a dubious bargain. In addition, good-quality, extended child care for before and after school was very limited. Private schools were a possibility, but paying as much for a year of kindergarten as we would for a year of college did not seem prudent.

To complicate matters, we wanted a second child. But the sheer logistics of juggling one child and two demanding careers were already more than we could handle. How could we justify a second child when we did not have enough time for our first? Like so many of our friends, we lived lives in which we pushed harder and ran faster in the vain hope of not falling too far behind. Would it be fair to bring one more child into our stopwatch world? We didn't think so. There simply weren't enough hours in the day—unless we significantly changed our lifestyles.

Housing

Housing in the city was another issue. We were still chasing the dream of owning our own house. But the harder we chased it, the more distant it seemed to become. Housing prices and taxes were rapidly rising, but our savings weren't. Then we came to a turning point. The house next door to the one we were renting came up for sale. The owners, who knew we were trying to buy our first home, offered to sell us the house significantly below market value if we would purchase it directly from them within thirty days. That way, they would be able to avoid the effort of showing the house and the expense of using a realtor.

We were ecstatic at first. *Homeowners at last!* we thought. We'd be able to get a house with a market value of $380,000 for $330,000! A bargain! But within a few days, doubt crept in. *A third of a million dollars? For a 3 BR, 1 BA house in an OK (but not great) neighborhood?* Wait a minute. Maybe we should think about this. *Sure it's less than they could get, but is a thirty-five-year-old suburban ranch house that needs work really worth a third of a million dollars?* Did we really want to go so deeply into mortgage slavery for something so minimal? Besides, whatever happened to the relationship between price and value?

The clincher came when Eric, who had grown up in a house only six blocks away and very similar to the one we were considering, discussed the situation with his father. One of Eric's earliest memories is his father complaining about the price he paid for that house. *This place was overpriced by a third. . . .* Eric called his father and asked just how much he had bought that house for in 1957. He was shocked by the answer: $17,000. Yes, there had been a lot of inflation since 1957. But the sobering reality was that houses once considered overpriced at $17,000 were now considered a bargain at $330,000. This realization, as much as any other, galvanized our decision to move to a small town.

Narrowing the Search to Smaller Towns

We knew we wanted to move, but deciding *where* soon became our biggest stumbling block. We didn't know how to go about looking for the right small town and we certainly didn't know how to go about agreeing on what to look for. When we first heard about the completion-backwards principle, we realized that it might offer us a starting point. It's a simple principle. First you determine where you want to end up, then you figure out in reverse the steps necessary to get there. Completion, for us, would be living in a town we really liked.

We changed tack and started asking people who really liked their towns just what it was that they liked. It was instantly apparent that this approach was far more effective than randomly casting about for information. Most people responded with specific attributes at first. *It's got a great hardware store. I'm only thirty minutes from good skiing. The fall here is beautiful.* When pressed, they tended to scrunch up their faces a little and make quite different points. *It's really friendly here . . . People know me . . . It has a good community feel . . . I feel like I matter here . . .*

In a world compulsively bent on measuring and quantifying, it was refreshing to find that people fell back on real but unmeasurable feelings to describe the things that mattered most to them. From this, we learned that if we were to find a place where we felt truly at home, our feelings were bound to play a major role.

When Eric conducted this informal survey of people who really liked where they lived, he noticed an interesting theme. Generally speaking, the smaller the community, the more people seemed to like where they were living. He came to the conclusion that the sheer size of a place was really important. One person is a bigger percentage of the population in a small town than in a city. The smaller a community, the more each person matters and the greater the effect each person can have.

....

Where there is an open mind, there will always be a frontier.

—Charles F. Kettering
Profile of America

Margaret was still reticent about small towns. She very much wanted to have a lifestyle that allowed her to participate in a community. She wanted to be more involved in the raising of our children, their schools, the neighborhood, and community issues. But small towns? Margaret liked the intellectual and cultural stimulus of a city. She wondered how much she would have to give up. She also questioned whether she would feel at home in a small community. At the time, her picture of small towns was limited to sleepy, isolated places with minimal activity. Her reticence began to ebb as she spoke with a large number of people leading fulfilling lives in small towns. The testimonial evidence was overwhelming.

Other, more tangible factors made small towns workable as well as appealing: the availability of overnight delivery services; advanced telecommunications; the rise of computer-based home and small businesses; increased job opportunities; diverse media availability. All of these are contributing to what we have come to believe is a quiet small-town renaissance.

Discovering the Right Approach

At about this time, we unconsciously began to shift our focus from the negative aspects of our current living situation to the positive aspects we sought in an ideal living environment. We had realized that simply finding a small town without the bad things we wished to escape wouldn't necessarily make it a good place to live. In addition to not having those bad things, it must have certain good things.

Our search for the right place to live became much more effective when we began to define the positive things we wanted to move to. This is one of the guiding premises of *My Kind of Town:* Seek the positive elements. Once we had defined our ideal small town, we began looking for information that would help us match our positive needs to one town in particular. When we decided to search for a place that had the things we wanted, as opposed to one that didn't have the things we didn't want, other search tactics fell rapidly into place.

We eventually realized that even working from an ideal model was not enough; in addition to a town having good things going for it, it had to *feel* right. There is a saying: *what you get is how you do it.* We knew we weren't going to end up in a place that felt right solely by designing and seeking some cold, rigid, statistical model of the perfect small town. Yes, we would need to base a significant part of our decision on hard factual information. But we also knew we needed to base our final choice on more than that. If it didn't *feel* right to us, it wouldn't *be* right for us. We needed a research and decision process that would give appropriate weight to both facts and feelings.

After many false starts, we finally arrived at a process that worked incredibly well. First we created our own criteria and standards. Then we used hard, quantifiable data to narrow the number of towns that matched those criteria. This done, we were able to make a final choice based on our feelings—secure in the knowledge that each town we were considering had already met the objective tests we had set. We refer to this process as hard-to-soft research. By this means, you answer the hard, factual, statistical questions early so that you can decide with your heart later.

It feels quite natural, and it works.

Choosing the Perfect Place

The definition of "small" is relative. To a New Yorker, Philadelphia is small. To a Philadelphian, Dayton, Ohio, is small. To a Daytonian, Flagstaff, Arizona, is small, and so on. Of course, size is hardly the only variable; there are tens of thousands of small communities in the United States, and even within a small region they can differ dramatically from each other. Some of them will be very appealing and livable. Others might not be.

There are also livable small cities. In fact, early in the process of evaluating our options we seriously considered moving to a smaller city rather than to a small town. There were several good reasons for us to consider the option. Margaret's career would be easier to pursue from a small city with an established computer and communications industry. Eric would have easier access to an airport with scheduled air service. In the end we opted for a small town because it proved to be the best, most workable option for us. For some people, small cities will be the best workable option. You may have careers, medical needs, or other requirements that simply cannot be met in a small town. If you are in this category, be assured there are some excellent small cities out there. This book is designed to be equally effective whether you are seeking the right small city or small town.

For our own purposes we eventually defined a town as small when it:
- Has a population less than about 25,000. (Larger than this and it would probably be too urban for us.)
- Is not in the obvious orbit of some other, larger urban area. (If it is, it would probably be too suburban for us.)
- Has a fairly self-sufficient economy.

- Is self-governing, with an obvious community and town center. (If it didn't have these, it would probably be too much of a sprawling strip or corridor for us.)

This is the loose definition we used in order to focus our own search. Your definition of a small town or city may be similar to ours or vastly different depending on your needs. This book will help you formulate your own parameters.

After many months, much research and cross-referencing, lots of discussions, and a few juicy arguments, we finally agreed on a shortlist of four small towns that best matched our unique needs. One by one, we visited them, and finally we made a choice.

This book is written from the small town we moved to. Was it the right move? Emphatically, yes. We chuckle when some people label us participants in—or victims of—the "domo" (downwardly mobile) trend because of our move to a small town. Our cost of living has decreased substantially. Our son is in a good public school, in a class of about twenty students. Our town is safe and friendly. Our library is open six days a week, and twelve hours a day for five of those days. We have free time (enough to write a book!) for the first time in years. We breathe clear air and drink clean water. Yet we live only one hour from a lively, attractive medium-sized city. The transition from urban area to small town has been easier than we ever imagined. In short, our lives are better. Much better.

We Supply the Process. You Supply the Goals.

In looking through this book you will not find the name of the small town we finally chose and moved to. It's not that we want to keep it secret. We'll welcome you with open arms if our book leads you to purchase the house next door to ours. The point is this: We found a place that is right for us. That does not mean that it will be right for you. *My Kind of Town* is intended to help you determine *your* needs and find a small town that meets them. This book can be used equally well by a family seeking a more traditional, family-oriented community and by a single woman or man seeking a small, liberal artist's community.

If you're dissatisfied with urban or suburban life and have not previously considered smaller communities as an option, perhaps our book will encourage you to take a look at them. They deserve it. In our own research we found few resources to help us evaluate the thousands of American small towns. This book is written to fill that void.

one

Thinking About
Small Towns

CHAPTER 1

The Small-Town
Renaissance

Since the day we started to consider relocating to a small town we have gradually become convinced that a quiet small-town renaissance is underway. In a world confronted with the images of its own decay on every nightly news broadcast, we have been amazed to find small, quiet corners of the nation where people see their lives actually improving—not just disintegrating less rapidly than the lives of others less fortunate than themselves.

At first, we did not recognize this small-town renaissance for what it was. We did not trust our perception that life in America's smaller communities was truly improving. We thought our view was skewed from our disenchantment with the urban/suburban grind. We distrusted our intuition and observations in the same way you distrust your sense of still being in motion when you first come to a stop after a long trip on the freeway. We thought that our perception had been poisoned by our perspective. We no longer do. At this point there is no doubt in our minds that many of America's small towns and small cities are very good places to live, and they are getting a little better every year.

The Scales Are Starting to Tip the Other Way

Until recently the American small town was seen as a dying species. The transition from the Agricultural Age to the Industrial Age, economic hardship, and the promise of opportunities in urban areas contributed to its decline. Until the 1940s the United States' demographic charts showed a steady flow from country to city. Over the ensuing decades some folks left the cities, but few returned to small towns. In the fifties and sixties, for example, people settled in vast nearby suburbs. During the late sixties and seventies, a few dropped out of city life to seek alternative lifestyles in rural areas. By the eighties, people returned to the cities once again, gentrifying the older, core neighborhoods. Each of these shifts had a common theme: People moved to places they believed would offer a better life.

....

I had a great job in New York, so I didn't mind it that much at the time. I would have stayed there, but it was tearing my husband apart. But I couldn't go back now. It'd be like putting a gun to my head. I know now how much it means to live someplace with a great lifestyle.

—Leigh P.

City	Population change since 1980
Birmingham, AL	- 6.5%
Denver, CO	- 5.1%
Bridgeport, CT	- 0.6%
Atlanta, GA	- 7.3%
Chicago, IL	- 7.4%
Louisville, KY	- 9.9%
New Orleans, LA	-10.9%
Baltimore, MD	- 6.4%
Detroit, MI	- 14.6%
Minneapolis, MN	- 0.7%
Jackson, MS	- 3.1%
Kansas City, MO	- 2.9%
Newark, NJ	- 16.4%
Philadelphia, PA	- 6.1%
Columbia, SC	- 3.1%
Salt Lake City, UT	- 1.9%
Charleston, WV	- 10.4%
Milwaukee, WI	- 1.3%

From 1980 to 1990, an amazing phenomenon occurred. During this decade the total population of the United States increased by 9.8 percent to over 248 million, but in more than one third (36 percent) of the individual states the largest city actually lost population. These figures are from the 1990 census, so they do not reflect the impact of the 1991 and 1992 massive defense cutbacks on the economies of many large cities, particularly in the West.

Warming Up to the Idea of Small Communities

Today, for the first time in many decades, it is the smaller communities of America that are capturing the attention of those seeking a better living environment. The course of our own story is quite typical. At first, Margaret just couldn't get her brain wrapped around the idea of leaving a major metropolitan area for some remote little town. So when we first began looking for a place to move, she looked at large university towns and small cities. This research opened her eyes to the vast number of different living environments available. From state to state, the nature of smaller cities varies widely. A small city in Texas is a very different place than one in California, Montana, New York, or Georgia—depending on its economic/industrial base, academic population, ethnic mix, traditions, and surroundings. Margaret realized that just because a small city had a university and a certain number of residents, it didn't necessarily offer what she wanted. Slowly the tether of preconceived notions weakened and she was drawn toward some radically different options. This, of course, was helped along by all those appealing bits and pieces of information about small towns that Eric kept waving under her nose.

Whether urban or suburban, some people will seek positive change in their lives without moving. They experiment with flextime, on-site child care, and compensation alternatives, such as additional vacation time in lieu of raises and bonuses. But for other people these measures are unavailable or inadequate. They amount to Band-Aids when major surgery is required.

Retirees are also moving out of urban America, taking their fixed incomes elsewhere. The lure of a lower cost of living, greater physical comfort, and the security of friendly neighbors is proving strong. In some areas of the country, retirees constitute the largest small-town population influx.

Small-Town Myths and Misconceptions

When we first started talking about trading in our urban existence for a small-town alternative, the reactions of friends and family ranged from the skeptical to the incredulous. Eric's father had fled Appalachia as soon as he had a freshly minted engineering degree to wave under the nose of any interested California employer. Both of Margaret's parents and Eric's mother were Los Angelenos who had moved to the San Francisco area. All were urbanites at heart. All loved their weekend trips to the country; all loved coming home to the city on Sunday night. None of them chose to live any place where population was measured in numbers of less than six figures.

Our parents' perspective was understandable. In their youth, many small towns really were forgotten backwaters. Their own parents were of the generation that fled the farm, and when they told stories of collapsing depression-era farm communities, they drew on bitter personal experience. Until a couple of decades ago, small towns offered precious few opportunities that didn't first require the purchase of a train ticket to the nearest large city.

The initial reaction of our friends was as skeptical as well, though the specific disadvantages they predicted were different. Here are some of the myths and misconceptions about small towns that we encountered before we moved, and our own experience with them.

Myth: *Small towns are politically conservative.* Yes, some small towns are very conservative. But then, some are very liberal. And most end up being about in the middle. They come in virtually any flavor you could imagine.

Myth: *Outsiders are only accepted after living in a small town for three generations.* We have found this particular myth to be among the most repeated, and among the least true. Our experience has been, like many émigrés we've talked with, that if you come to a small community and demonstrate a willingness to contribute—to put something "into the pot"—you will quickly be accepted. We have heard of few cases where this has not proved true.

Myth: *In a small town everybody knows your business.* It's not that small-town people are more nosy, it's that they are less anonymous. In a small community, you interact more frequently with a smaller number of people. It's inevitable that you will get to know each other better in the process. The better you know someone, the more of their "business" you know. And vice versa. Our son makes sure our elderly neighbor with arthritis doesn't have to go into the snow to get her newspaper. And she keeps an eye on our house when we're gone. Do we know each other's business? Yes, to a certain extent we do. But we wouldn't have it any other way.

Myth: *Small towns are homogenous and boring.* It may have been true in the past, but for an increasing number of small towns, this too is a modern-day myth. Many small towns are gaining diversity and personality at the same time that many urban or suburban areas are losing it. For instance, we hear people claim that there are no good restaurants in small towns. In our experience, if you look carefully, you'll find restaurants that are some of America's best tucked into out-of-the-way villages and towns. A wonderful restaurant near us makes a plate of smoked salmon with cracked pepper that is one of the most delicious culinary treats we've eaten anywhere.

In small towns and small cities you'll find local arts and crafts co-ops, lecture series, music festivals, harvest fairs, and rodeos. We predict you'll discover—as we did—that diverse and interesting places now come in small packages.

Myth: *Small towns suffocate children.* This has not been our experience. Our son Douglas may be swimming in a smaller pond, but here he comes into contact with all types of fish rather than the homogenous suburban species he was exposed to before. Now, just as before, it is our responsibility as parents to see that he is exposed to a broad range of ideas and perspectives. If anything, in a small town he has greater access because he has the freedom to roam and wander.

Myth: *Small-town schools are unable to prepare children for college.* There are some excellent small-town school districts and some poor ones. Some high schools have good college prep programs while others have none, just like in cities. But here's one big difference we've found. The level of violence and intimidation in most small-town schools is much lower than in urban schools. Your child can concentrate on chemistry class in the morning instead of worrying how to make it home safely that afternoon.

Myth: *Small towns are bigoted and intolerant.* Worst case? Yes. There are some small towns that are quite bigoted and intolerant—and as recent events have demonstrated, some of our largest cities fit that description equally well. Both of us have heard a few really ugly remarks on occasion, just as we had before moving out of the city. We see a difference in small towns, though. In a small community, it's harder to be ugly because it's harder to be anonymous. It's harder to treat somebody harshly if you know you will see them every few days in the market, at the gas station, or at little league practice.

Myth: *There's nothing productive for teenagers to do in small towns.* Not true, from what we've seen. Here are the extracurricular activities of a few of the teenagers we know in our town: One interned as a trainee software designer at a local electronics company that is developing the next generation of electronic aircraft landing systems. In our town's volunteer fire department, there are several high school students (both boys and girls) who are trainee firefighters. A few have even completed basic paramedic training. Other teenagers work in the local orchards. Many are involved in team and individual sports. Then there are the local youth theater and music events, 4-H, the County Fair, and environmental youth task groups.

Myth: *Everyone's poor in small towns.* While it may be true that average small-town incomes are lower, it is certainly true that average small-town expenses are lower. Ask yourself: if both your income and your expenses drop by 20 percent, are you poorer or richer? If your quality of life goes up at the same time as your income and expenses drop by 20 percent, aren't you better off than before?

. . . .

Our daughter Sara had a great deal of trepidation to begin with in our new town—the kids were more rowdy and the environment more free form. But she made friends really easily and she can go to the library, the store, and other places by herself here. The amount of independence has really boosted her self-esteem.

—Sandi F.

It's not fair that small towns are seen to live in the shadows of their own pasts, but they are. One of the obstacles you're likely to face when exploring the idea of moving to a new place is the misperception that small towns are limiting and limited. Lots of people would have you believe that *all* small towns are isolated backwaters suffering in abject poverty. They're not. By the end of your search process you'll discover, as we have, that thousands of today's small towns have a lot to offer. In fact, with equal amounts of planning, creativity, and flexibility, you may find that you can make a better living in a small town than where you live now. You can certainly enjoy a higher quality of life while doing so.

Many of these myths have their roots in past truths or half truths. But the world has changed, and small communities have changed with it.

What Small Towns Are Like Today

Backwoods no longer means backwards. *Peyton Place* was one of many stereotypic descriptions of the small towns of several decades ago. At that time, small towns were often thought of as isolated and unsophisticated. It may have been true then. It is not true today. Even the most remote houses can now have satellite dishes that receive the same television programming (albeit of the same dubious quality) available to any big-city resident. UPS and FedEx deliver to almost every small town in the United States. Many small country inns offer excellent menus with farm-fresh ingredients and low prices. For every big urban symphony orchestra on the verge of bankruptcy there are dozens of thriving local or regional music festivals.

For the most part smaller communities have retained their friendly townishness but gained enormously in sophistication, accessibility, and resources. The following is a look at the specific advantages that smaller communities offer today.

Healthier Economies. If the economy of the 1990s continues to be the roller coaster ride some analysts are predicting, small towns may prove to be a much sought-after safe haven. Thanks to simpler infrastructures, increasingly diverse employment opportunities, and the influx of income from recent urban transplants, the smaller towns of the 1990s are looking healthier than their larger urban counterparts.

Small towns can run on a leaner budget than cities. They don't need the enormous infrastructure that a big city does, so when portions of a small town's infrastructure do need repair, replacement, or expansion, the cost is not so staggering. The lack of state and federal support

....

There was a racial incident where my daughters were called "niggers." I wrote a letter that day to the town paper, asking parents to talk to their kids about racism. The response by the community was wonderful. They talked to their kids. People cut the newspaper article out and pasted it in their storefronts downtown to say, "We won't tolerate this." No way would there have been a community response back in Detroit on this scale.

—Kesho S.

that some small-town governments have complained bitterly about in the past may turn out to have been a blessing in disguise. Small towns will enjoy the benefits of self-sufficiency in the future because they were forced to learn the skill in the past.

During past periods of economic hardship, regional and local govern-ments and industries learned the hard way that survival meant diversification. As a result, many small towns have taken steps to encourage multiple sources of revenue. A steel or lumber town, for example, now might have a growing electronics or tourism business as well. This has helped prevent the devastating unemployment that literally made ghosts of small towns in the past.

This combination of self-reliance and a revitalized openness to new opportunities puts small towns in a better position to weather economic bad times.

Equal Access to Modern Technology. The *global village* concept refers to the idea that today's technology connects us with a community of other people who are not necessarily in our immediate environment. This technology frees us from the confines of our local surroundings; we can extend our businesses, our jobs, and our pleasures to the far corners of the world. We can live as far away from urban centers as we want and communicate with others in equally remote locations. So our sense of community, of village, comes from mutual interests on a global level and is no longer limited to what's available on a merely local level.

Modern telecommunications, faxes, computers, modems, fast mail services, electronic mail, and electronic bulletin boards make it possible to view living in a small town in a new light. No longer must small-town residents drive hours to see a movie, to watch a professional ball game, or to shop. Cable TV, video stores, and satellite and microwave communi-cations deliver access to the same services urban residents have. Express delivery services, 800 telephone numbers, and fax machines have made it possible to order directly from major department and specialty stores. Direct-mail businesses have boomed, and merchandise ordered now arrives in a matter of days, rather than weeks.

Electronic communications have also made it easier to pursue special interests and to participate in associations and clubs previously only found in metropolitan areas. Discussion forums on electronic bulletin boards cover just about any topic imaginable, from computer user tips to the latest art, music, and political trends. Stock prices and other financial indicators are available through such on-line services as CompuServe®, Prodigy®, America On-Line®, and Dow Jones

News/Retrieval®. Financial transactions can often be conducted electronically, as well.

Perhaps most important is the fact that new technologies have opened the doors for new employment opportunities and new ways of working. For an in-depth discussion of this topic, turn to Chapter 2, Can You Really Make a Living in a Small Town?

Financial Advantages. Another factor to think about when looking at small-town employment opportunities is the relative cost of living, particularly if you currently live in an urban area. Lower housing costs, fewer expenses, and a simpler lifestyle add up to less overhead. This lower cost of living gives you greater flexibility in how much money you need to earn and *how* you earn a living. You may find you have some employment choices in a small town that wouldn't be possible elsewhere, simply because you can afford to earn less.

For us, moving to a small town meant being able to live well on only one income. The cost of housing made the biggest difference. In the city, our monthly rent was a major load. There was little hope of being able to actually buy a house. When we moved we were finally able to buy a house that is larger than the one we were renting and with a monthly mortgage that is half what we had been paying in rent. Our driving has decreased significantly, since Margaret works from a home studio. Our gas, parking, and insurance expenses have dropped. Other expenses for services, such as dry cleaning, eating a lot of take-out, and extended day care, are practically nil.

Our whole approach to earning a living has changed because our income/expense cycle is radically different. We have fewer expenses and lower expenses. This means we can enjoy a better quality of life on less money, which in turn means we have more time and freedom to pursue creative projects that are important to us but that might not bring an immediate financial return (the writing of this book, for instance). The result, for us, is the opportunity to pursue our creative endeavors while enjoying a higher overall quality of living. Whether it's artistic pursuits, a yen to take the summer off with the kids, or time to tinker with building a better mousetrap, the reality is that we all need a financial situation and lifestyle that permit us to do more than spend most of our waking hours working and commuting.

Life on a Human Scale. The more people we spoke with, the more convinced we became that the sheer size of a community is a critical factor.

While people in small towns invariably spoke to us glowingly of their environs, people in cities seemed to grumble about them. A psychologist might have elaborate explanations to offer, but a simple one is sufficient. People want to matter. In a city, an individual is just one more blank face in a crowd of millions, give or take a few hundred thousand. In a small town, you're somebody.

People want to have an impact on their communities, to feel they can effect change when they are dissatisfied with their environment. Here's a hypothetical example. Let's say that you live in a city of five hundred thousand. As cities go, it is not all that large. Let's also say that 20 percent of the total populace votes regularly. That makes a hundred thousand voters. You enter the picture and want to pursue a local political issue. You decide you would like to organize a political rally of the active voters. In order to do so you must fill a football stadium and make your speech, and not once, but several times. Given these obstacles, it is no wonder that the civic affairs of most cities are run by unapproachable professional politicians with access to enormous sums of money. Sadly, there is little chance for the individual citizen to make his or her voice heard.

Now let's say you live in a small town with a population of five thousand, of which one thousand are active voters. To speak directly to voters in your town, you could probably use the local high school gymnasium. Here, even the average citizen can have a voice, can have an impact, and can matter.

Small towns operate on a human scale. Unlike the feeling of helplessness that city life fosters, you feel your influence in a small town and have some control over your environment.

Community and Family Atmosphere. There are many aspects of small-town life—the community spirit, friendliness, and closeness—in which a small town is different simply because of its scale. There your influence and involvement extend to schools, events, and local and regional planning. If there is a problem or threat of any kind, citizens in a small community can organize and respond quickly.

You also have greater control over your children's lives: education, safety, and upbringing. People in small towns take the time to get to know each other. Chances are your child's teacher is a neighbor, or goes to your church. The local police and fire forces are often made up in part of volunteers, some of whom are also your neighbors. The local store-keeper, music teacher, and swim coach are all familiar faces around town.

Slower, Healthier Pace. Consider the impact of exchanging a 45-minute one-way commute (that's 1 hour and 30 minutes every day, a relatively short commute by contemporary urban standards) for a 5-minute one-way commute (that's 10 minutes daily) in a small town. You have an extra 1 hour and 20 minutes every day to do something you enjoy. That's not bad. The impact is more pronounced if you think of it on a weekly basis. Every week you will have 6 hours and 40 minutes of free time you didn't have before. Let's assume that you work 50 weeks a year. That decrease in your daily commute length just gained you 13 days, 21 hours, and 20 minutes of free time through the course of your work year. Think of it as that much more vacation time. That's exactly what it is.

What You Gain by Shortening Your Commute

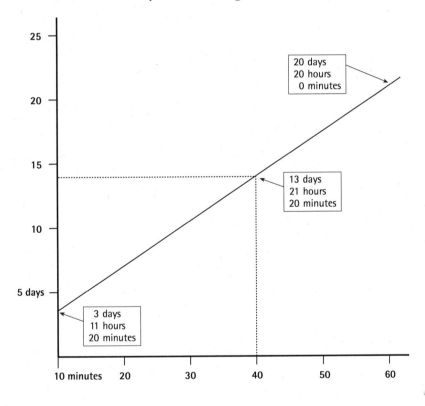

If you save the minutes counted across the bottom of this graph on each commute, you gain the days of free time per year that are counted up the left side.

Maybe small towns are friendlier because people are willing to
sacrifice a little of their extra 13 days, 21 hours, and 20 minutes (to use
our example) to be courteous and warm. Some small towns have very
slow paces, others are more energetic. Not one of the towns we explored,
however, suffered from the "hurry-up-and-wait" syndrome. Maybe a
small town's pace is slower because there is simply no need for it to be
so fast. There is logic to the saying, *Slow down, you'll get more done.*

In small towns, smelling the roses, spending time with families,
friends, and neighbors, or enjoying the surroundings is not just an occa-
sional indulgence. It's a way of life.

Is a Small Town for You?

We've described above a few typical characteristics of many of
today's small towns. If the lifestyle portrayed appeals to you, then the
answer to whether a small town is for you is very likely yes.

Whatever you're looking for, there is an excellent chance that it's
out there somewhere. There are tens of thousands of small towns in
the United States. Some are close to skiing. Some have no-growth
planning codes. Some are staunchly conservative. Some are near excellent
fishing. Some are host to colleges and universities. Some are quite
modern. Some are county seats. Some are liberal artists' enclaves.
Some have excellent schools. Some have a strong ethnic presence.
Some have a beautiful old Main Street. The point is, each one of them
has a lot to offer to the right person.

No matter how apparently contradictory, rigorous, or specific your
desires and needs are, there is most likely a small town somewhere out
there in the vastness and variety of the United States that will satisfy them.
The most important goal, then, is to be very sure you select the small
town that is right for you. Our aim in writing this book is to help you do
just that. The next chapter takes an in-depth look at the employment
issues you'll face in moving to a small town, and the opportunities and
solutions that are available today.

CHAPTER 2

Can You Really Make a Living
in a Small Town?

Yes, in the vast majority of cases, you can. It might mean some compromises. It might require a new approach to working at your existing job. Or it might even mean starting your own business. In the most extreme cases, it might mean a change in the type of work you do. But there is a wealth of new ways of earning a living in today's small communities.

The employment opportunities in—and *from*—small towns are much broader than they used to be. New technology, in particular, is changing the face of small-town employment. It is now possible to telecommute, run a global business from remote headquarters, or consult from afar. Making a living independent of a small community economy is possible in ways that simply didn't exist ten years ago. If you can't find the job you want locally, you may be able to create one that is not dependent on the local marketplace.

Fortunately, in many small cities and towns the local economic scene has changed a lot as well. If the new-tech, global-village work-style isn't for you, don't worry. You'll be surprised at how many small towns today have employment opportunities that match your skills. This is, in large part, because many small towns learned their lessons from the last economic down-turn and are diversifying their economies. The "company" town that used to depend on one industry such as lumber or steel is fading into the sunset. Small towns are realizing the benefits of multiple industries. The result is a greater selection of jobs.

The town we live in, for example, used to be heavily dependent on its orchard and timber industries. These industries still exist, but over the last ten years the town has expanded its tourism industry and encouraged high technology, publishing, sports-equipment manufacturing, and other types of new businesses to move in. Most of the new businesses are not solely dependent on local markets, but they all employ local people.

Other factors are also converging to stimulate small-town economies and greater employment opportunities. Here are a few of these trends:

....

Small towns are a new frontier for minority and women professionals. The town I live in has five doctors of color.

—Kesho S.

• More and more people are relocating to small towns, bringing new skills and fresh energy. Many of these people are arriving with their own businesses, or starting new businesses once they arrive. Others have the skills or financial resources to help existing businesses expand.

• The information superhighway is making it possible for employees and independent consultants to earn a living miles away from their employers or customers. This is a trend that has only just begun.

• The information superhighway is also making it increasingly efficient for businesses to relocate to small-town areas where the costs of living and labor are often lower.

• Retirees are creating a whole array of new job and business opportunities in small towns. They are flocking to small towns, bringing with them a need for new kinds of businesses, such as specialized health and financial services.

• Many states are actively investing in small-town business development and diversification. They are offering tax incentives to encourage businesses from other areas to relocate. States are raising funds through lotteries and other channels for economic growth and business development. Much of this funding is going toward the seeding of small businesses in nonurban areas.

All these factors are increasing the number of opportunities for earning a living in, or from, a small town. That's not to say every small town in the United States is growing or even thriving. Not all are. Some have gathered another layer of ghost-town dust as you read this sentence. Realistically, there might not be the breadth of choice in your favorite small-town area that exists in a major metropolitan area. However, there may be fewer trade-offs than you think.

This chapter explores the trends that are increasing small-town employment options and how you can take advantage of them. It discusses alternative workstyles and presents some issues that you'll want to ponder when considering your employment options. Later, Chapter 6 will give you a means to sort through your particular employment situation, assess your unique needs and desires, and help you arrive at a range of possible work options.

What Kind of Success Do You Really Want?

Before you begin exploring your small-town work options, take a moment to think about why you are considering the move to a small town at all. For many, relocating to a small town is part of a quest for a better balance of work and play. It's the desire for a lifestyle that promises a healthy balance of job, friends, family, hobbies, leisure, and fun. In order to achieve this balanced lifestyle, however, you may have to make some significant changes in how you earn a living. You may have to redefine success in your own mind.

Two Ways to Spend Your Days

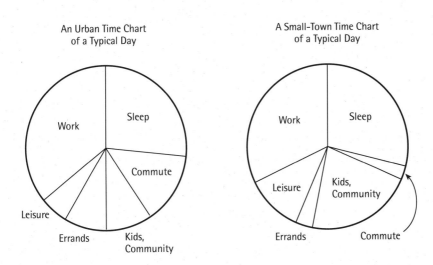

An Urban Time Chart
of a Typical Day

A Small-Town Time Chart
of a Typical Day

People are finding that small towns are more conducive to living a well-balanced life.

The concept of work is fundamentally different in a small town than in urban areas. In small towns, life tends to come first. People go home for lunch. They take time to acknowledge each other. They are up front with their employers and coworkers about their personal lives and family demands. Work is just one slice of life's pie—not the whole pie. It's a different approach.

If you are hooked on the frenetic stimulus of working on the floor of the New York Stock Exchange or on the studio set of a Hollywood TV sitcom, ask yourself whether the slower pace of a small town, even if saner, could make you happy. (Then again, if you're that attached to the thrill of continuous frenzy, mania, and pandemonium, you're probably not reading this book.)

Look carefully at the towns you consider moving to and the values you want to maintain. Small-town priorities and values can be very different from urban ones.

Making the Most of a Career Transition

Moving to a small town can be especially appealing if you're at a time of transition, such as a major career change, early retirement, or lay-off. This is a great time to rethink what you want out of life. Consider the full extent of your options. Is there really any reason to look for the same old job in the same old living environment?

Let your mind wander back to the career ideas of earlier days. Do you still dream of having a small business making custom flies for fishing, or writing children's books, or owning a small hardware store? Or perhaps you always wanted to go back to school to train for an entirely different field. This might be an excellent time to pursue a new path.

There Are Many Ways to Earn a Living

Rekindle your earlier dreams. Keep an open mind to ways of earning a living that are radically different from your current situation. Explore your options. There are many ways to search beyond your current field of employment. You can:

- Talk to people in a wide variety of professions and find out what they like and dislike about what they're doing.
- Go to a career counselor and assess your unique skill set.
- Go back to school for some additional training.
- Try out a new field through an internship or temporary contract work.
- Volunteer to help a local nonprofit organization that supports a field of your interest.
- Contact your local Small Business Administration office for information and a list of workshops on small business and franchise ownership.

What's Possible?

Not only does the world come to small towns—through television, radio, mail, and improved transportation—but now small towns can easily reach out to the world.

Anyone living in a small town today can communicate with clients, business partners, and vendors via fax, phone, express mail, electronic mail, teleconferencing, and even videoconferencing. You can send data over modems and high-speed digital data lines. You can purchase parts from different manufacturers around the world, assemble them in one location, and distribute them from another. You can ship product to anywhere in the world.

Even a small town as remote as Lusk, Wyoming, (population just over fifteen hundred) is being wired with fiber optic cable by U.S. West. With this kind of high bandwidth cabling and digital switches, the townsfolk of Lusk will be able to connect electronically to business, government, and private entities anywhere in the world. The business opportunities that arise from this advanced technology give Lusk a competitive edge over other, much larger towns.

Virtual Corporations and Project Workers

The structure of corporations is becoming more loosely defined, spawning new kinds of entities, such as the *virtual corporation*. What is a virtual corporation? Imagine a company with only one or two employees. All of its essential functions, like manufacturing, warehousing, distribution, sales, advertising, and bookkeeping, are performed by firms or individuals, sometimes scattered across the nation, who work as independent contractors. There are virtual corporations with sales of over $10 million a year and only one employee—the owner. By the extensive use of outside contractors and consultants, the virtual corporation can remain incredibly flexible and at the same time keep its overhead to an absolute minimum. Participating in such a structure, as either the owner or a contractor, can work well for people who want to live in small towns and work for themselves.

Today's technology makes it possible for virtual and conventional corporations to bring together the geographically dispersed teams of contractors—project workers—who best suit particular jobs. Corporations can fax work to a specialized labor pool at a remote location across the country or overseas, and have it back the next morning.

An increasing number of companies are finding that this approach to doing business can be cost-efficient and yield better and faster results than using full-time, on-site staff employees. It's enabled many corporations to relocate part or all of their businesses outside of metropolitan areas.

....

... technology is helping distribute economic power throughout the American landscape. Major advances in telecommunications are creating a footloose economy that permits firms to locate where they want to be, not where the traditional centers of finance and commerce dictate they have to be. In short, the economic deck is being reshuffled.

—David A. Heenan,
The New Corporate Frontier: The Big Move to Small Town U.S.A.

Virtual Corporations: The Wave of Today

Journal Graphics, a virtual corporation, has no traditional headquarters. This company sells transcripts of television shows and has a mailing address in Denver, but its employees work out of their homes, taping shows on personal VCRs and transcribing them on home computers. The material is directly uploaded to satellite channels, FM digital networks, and on-line data networks, and subscribers can access it within hours of the show.

Unifi Communications Corp. in Billerica, Massachusetts, is helping the trend by selling a system that automatically routes customer service calls to employees in different parts of the country. A company can have 800 numbers that are staffed by people working out of their homes, in a variety of locations and time zones.
—The above examples are from "The Virtual Workplace," by David C. Churbuck and Jeffrey S. Young, *Forbes,* November 23, 1992.

Taking Advantage of the Emerging Possibilities

How do *you* tie into this network? Where is your on-ramp to the information superhighway? Let's look at a hypothetical example of a virtual corporation and number some of the services and functions it requires. Each one offers an opportunity for you to ally yourself with the corporation. PoweRV Inc. is a recreational-vehicle accessory company located in a small town. Its product is a specialized power supply cord assembly that enables a visiting RV to park in a host's driveway and safely connect to the host's household electrical system. In those instances when an RV might be parked in a host's driveway for a long period of time, like a prolonged visit to see children, this accessory keeps the RV's generator from kicking on in the middle of the night and annoying the neighbors. It is a small niche market, but sales are brisk.

The owners, Bob and Fran, have good managerial skills (1). They outsource everything else. They contract out product design (2) and complex prototype development and product testing to different companies (3), depending on the materials involved. The manufacturing is done in a small plant several states away (4). Their marketing and advertising materials are written and designed by a local freelancer (5) and printed at a company (6) in another state. The distribution of their products is handled in part through a contract mail-order processing service (7) and in part by a small, regional distribution agency (8). They use a contract warehouse service (9) that ships the units on instructions from their mail-order service. In one business, here are nine opportunities for project workers.

Bob and Fran split their time between their small town home and prolonged trips, always part sales trips, in their own plush RV. With fax, phone, and modem, they can run their virtual corporation from the comfort of their RV while it is parked in one or another of their children's driveways, often a thousand miles from home. Their customers and suppliers would never guess that they were not working out of their usual office (which actually happens to be in a corner of their living room).

There are many opportunities to step up to the electronic well. You could be the one spearheading a virtual company, or you could be one of those providing contract or subcontract services or parts, from wherever you happen to be located.

Electronic communication has opened up new opportunities for direct-mail entrepreneurs as well. Similar to the RV-accessories example cited above, you can situate a direct-mail business in a small town and sell your products to a wide market of geographically dispersed customers

A Hypothetical Virtual Corporation

Product Manufacturer
(4)

Products Shipped
by Truck

Overnight
Package Service

Final Design by Modem

Product Designer
(2)

Prototype & Testing
(3)

Instructions by Fax

The PoweRV Company
(1)

Ideas by Phone/Fax

Products Shipped
by Rail

Specifications by Fax

Freelance Catalog Designer
(5)

Distributor
(8)

Payment

Truck

Warehouse & Shipping
(9)

Truck

Overnight Mail

R.V. Equipment Sales

Order
Shipped by
UPS

Printing Company
(6)

Customer Takes

Payment

Order Transmitted by Modem

The Customer

Mail-Order Processing
(7)

Telephone Order

This is what the PoweRV Company really looks like. Most of its suppliers are like its customers—they are thousands of miles from the PoweRV Company itself. These days, location matters little. Each one could be in a small town in any state. Where can you plug in? Anywhere your skills and energy allow. Hint: Don't just think of plugging into the boxes—think about what you can do to connect or merge the boxes.

who order via an 800 number or fax. More and more people are shopping from home. Today's technology and rapid shipping make it easy and fast to send products to customers, no matter where they live. Electronic on-line and interactive television approaches to home shopping are gaining popularity as well. These technologies will make it even easier to reach customers, no matter where your business is located.

Our Workstyles Are Changing, Too

The nine-to-five workday is going the same way as carbon paper, for both employees and employers. Large employers are reacting to increasing competition by pushing their employees to work harder and longer hours. Concurrently the same megacorporations are telling their employees not to expect secure, long-term employment. Meanwhile the employee base in this country is aging, and the traditional workday no longer fits huge sectors of our population.

The baby boomers, with their own boomlet of children, are increasingly torn between work and family. Single parents are anguishing over lousy day care and lack of time with their youngsters. Retirees are living longer and finding that they want or need to earn postretirement income. Increasingly, Americans are striving to balance their work lives with their nonwork lives. They want time for community service, family, and creative and leisure pursuits.

Fortunately, many companies are seeing the light. They are realizing that in order to keep valuable employees, they must become more flexible. And, of course, they are encouraged by the positive effects that alternative work arrangements can have on their bottom lines. They are embracing the idea that workforce and workplace flexibility can help them meet the challenges of a highly competitive, global economy.

Alternatives to the Traditional Nine-to-Five

Flexible work arrangements such as telecommuting, compressed work weeks, flexiplace, flextime, job sharing, part-time work, and interim employment are increasing in popularity. These new workstyles can meet the needs of both wage earners and employers. How can you take advantage of these workstyle alternatives? And what do they have to do with small towns? The following is a look at how nontraditional workstyles can make it possible to live far away from your employer. In Chapter 6, you'll have a chance to evaluate these options in relation to your own skills and needs.

Achievement without exhaustion. Accomplishment with less stress.

—Faith Popcorn,
The Popcorn Report
on trends in the
nineties

For many, new opportunities will be based in home offices instead of traditional office parks. The synergy of technology and communications is enabling this fundamental shift, and it will change forever our definition of what a workplace is.

—Maggie Canon,
Editor-in-Chief,
MacUser

New Self-Employment Opportunities. Today's technology is making an enormous difference in how and *where* we work. You can be an entrepreneur, an independent contractor, or a consultant, working at a location far away from where your clients or customers are located. At the heart of this approach is the notion that we can take our skills with us, working from a "home base" of our own choosing, and traveling if and when necessary.

Home-based businesses are no longer limited to taking in laundry, stuffing envelopes, or building widgets in the garage. You don't have to be a computer programmer, either, even though many of today's jobs involve, at least in part, some computer use.

	Information-Age Jobs
Many jobs can be done from the location of your choosing, thanks to today's electronic technologies. Among them are: Accounting, architectural design, bookkeeping, cartography, computer-aided design, computer programming, consumer consulting, credit checking, data entry, data processing, data research, desktop publishing, desktop video production, documentation, drafting, editing, electronic consulting, fabric design, fashion design, financial services, foreign language translation, graphic design, genealogy, illustration, insurance claims adjusting, insurance consulting, landscape design, legal transcription, lobbying, marketing services, medical transcription, music composing, on-line consulting, photography touch-up services, researching, remote systems analysis, sales, tax preparation, telemarketing, technical documentation, technical translation, technical writing, travel arrangement, word processing, writing.	

Small-Business Opportunities. If you want to relocate a small business, you'll face a more complex set of questions and issues. You'll need to ask yourself questions like these:

- Can I afford to move all or some of my current employees who must be physically present?
- If not, will any of my current employees be willing to move themselves in order to stay with my wonderful company and gain the advantage of living in a small town?
- Are there people with the right skill set whom I could hire in the small town I want to relocate to?
- Are there opportunities for training people in the small town I'm considering?
- What about my clients or customers? Will I be able to take them with me or must I plan on rebuilding some portion of my business in a new location?

- What about office space or a good plant location? Will I be able to find the right type of space?

Don't underestimate the possibilities of hiring good talent in small towns. More and more talented workers are moving to nonurban areas, bringing exceptional skills with them. In our town, we continue to meet people with an incredible array of skills and experience. The range of skills is impressive, from computer specialists to artists, audio engineers and film editors to political consultants, and more.

In the Resource Appendix at the end of the book, you will find a list of excellent books on starting your own business.

Greater Corporate Employment Opportunities. Today, more and more large companies are moving their businesses to small-town areas, providing a new array of corporate employment opportunities. The high cost of urban office space and labor, higher employee stress and health problems, and countless lost hours wasted on grid-locked freeways make small towns appealing to many metropolitan companies. They are relocating their service and manufacturing divisions to less-populated areas because they simply don't need to be in population centers any longer. The companies often agree to hire locally in exchange for state and local tax breaks. This trend is increasing the number of corporate job opportunities in many small-town areas.

Big Corporations Move to Small Towns	According to a poll by *Fortune* magazine, 73 percent of chief executives of the Fortune 500 companies said that they had relocated some facilities between 1985 and 1990 to nonmetropolitan areas. Eighty-one percent expect to relocate facilities in the future. This has opened up new job opportunities that allow many professionals to use their skills in nonurban areas for the first time. For example, Apple Computer now has a manufacturing site in Colorado Springs. J.C. Penny relocated three thousand employees from New York City to Plano, Texas. Sony is planning a manufacturing site in Springfield, Oregon. And the list goes on.

New Workstyles for Employees. What if you hate where you live but love your job? Or if your work is very specialized and only found in large cities? Or if you're just a few years away from retirement and a well-deserved pension for a firmly entrenched urban company? None of these is a reason to dismiss the idea of moving to a small town. Just because your job is in a city or suburb, *you* may not have to be.

Nah, my employer will never go for it, you might be saying to yourself. Well, maybe not. But did you know that the majority of American companies are now offering some form of alternative work arrangements? The number of workers on alternative work schedules has risen sharply over the past five years. According to the technology research and consulting firm Link Resources, in 1993 over 41 million Americans were working part or full time from home offices, using a computer, modem, fax, multiple phone lines, or some combination of these.

Here's a closer look at several increasingly popular alternative workstyles:

Telecommuting. The once futuristic predictions that employees and independent contractors could work from home or from satellite offices are finally becoming a reality. The number of workers telecommuting has been increasing 15–20 percent per year since 1990. Studies have shown that, counter to initial fears, the productivity rate of employees who are telecommuting actually rises. According to the San Francisco nonprofit agency New Ways to Work, most employers report significant productivity gains among their telecommuting employees due to fewer distractions and increased motivation. Telecommuting also reduces a company's need for costly office space.

Once the switch is made from staff work to earning a living as a telecommuting independent contractor, success depends in large part on having good communication with clients, whether this involves travel for face-to-face meetings or electronic communications. Those who take their Rolodexes with them to small towns are a step ahead if they continue to do work, long-distance, for employers and customers with whom they already have established relationships.

Part-time Employment and Job Sharing. If you move to a small town not too far away, you might consider staying in your current job on a part-time basis to provide short-term steady income while you establish a means of earning a living in your new hometown. Or it can provide a workable long-term strategy if combined with telecommuting. If a part-time job in your current company is not readily available, consider creating one by proposing a job-share arrangement.

A job share usually works something like this: you and an equally skilled person divide a job in half. The divvying up can be based on projects, clients, geographic responsibility, or simply on a schedule. When

From 1960 to 1990, an astonishing two-thirds of U.S. Fortune 500 companies head-quartered in New York City left town. . . . Corporate America's next frontier? Out of town, all the way! Look for more and more farsighted businesses to leapfrog the megalopolis—and in one dramatic move settle in grass-roots America.

—David A. Heenan, *The New Corporate Frontier: The Big Move to Small Town U.S.A.*

the basis is a schedule, usually each person works half of each day or half of each week, alternating two days one week, three days the next. This can work out really well, especially if you have good rapport with your job-share partner. (It's not dissimilar to having a housemate. If you're a neatnik and your housemate thinks washing the dishes is something that ought to be done every couple of weeks, beware.) Another advantage to job-sharing is that there are often more skilled full-time positions to choose from than part-time ones. A job share might mean greater opportunity to work at your skill level.

More and more companies are willing to give these kinds of alternative work arrangements a try. In fact, over two-thirds of all companies employ part-time employees today. Twelve to 20 percent of companies offer job sharing. Many of these positions carry at least some medical and retirement benefits.

Compressed Work Weeks and Flextime. If you're locked into full-time work, flextime and compressed work-week arrangements might help make it possible to stay in your current job and live in a small town several hours away. Compressed work weeks have been around for a long time. In fact, some professions are based on this kind of work schedule. Airline pilots, stewardesses, marine engineers, medical professionals, and many others have had compressed schedules for decades. Four days on, three days off. Three days on, four days off. Two weeks on, two weeks off. You get the picture. An extreme example is Eric's schedule as a merchant ship officer, gone for four months and back for three.

Flextime usually refers to having some flexibility about when you start and stop your job each day. For instance, you might work seven to three one week, and nine to five the next. Or, if the type of work permits, you might have the option of arriving at any time at all, as long as you put in a full day once you get there. Urban companies have been giving flextime a try in order to help their employees avoid rush hours. Also, many companies are recognizing that in families where both parents work, or where there is only one parent, this kind of flexibility is sorely needed.

Flextime and compressed work weeks can be good transitional steps if you don't want to quit your current job outright. These options can make it possible to drive, take a train or bus, or fly in from a small town several hours away. It might take some extra creativity to make this kind of alternative work arrangement succeed. It's not for everyone.

....

It's a negotiation process. People negotiate salary, help for relocation, benefits. Alternative work arrangements are one more thing that people are starting to negotiate for.

—Barney Olmstead, founder of the consulting organization New Ways to Work in San Francisco

....

We figured if we have to commute, we'd rather commute in the country where it's beautiful.

—Page C.

You'll need to consider: Where do you stay? Do you have to maintain two living places? What happens if you are asked to put in overtime at the office? What if your three-day compressed work week keeps stretching into four or five days? Is telecommuting for part of your total weekly work hours a realistic possibility? Commuting from a small town for three hours, three days a week, versus across town for one and a half hours, five days a week, isn't exactly a bargain.

Nonstaff Alternatives. The Conference Board, a nonprofit organization that researches business enterprises, has estimated that nearly one third of the workforce is employed as "contingent" workers, also called "non-staff." These are people who are full- or part-time temporary workers, consultants, independent contractors, special project workers, and so on. They include people who are working from home and who are self employed.

One fast-growing area of nonstaff work is "interim employment." Unlike traditional temporary work, which brings to mind secretarial, clerical, and moving-company jobs, interim employment usually is professional, specialist, and management-level jobs. For example, an interim employment agency might provide a company with an experienced professional or team of professionals to work on a specific assignment, such as implementing a quality-assurance strategy or revamping an operations process. The project might last a few weeks or many months. It often requires working on-site. This style of employment works well if you're willing to live away from home for periods of time.

Transferable Skills. Sometimes it's difficult to see beyond your current job, or place of employment. If you're feeling locked in to your job, now might be the time to reach for the mental key. One way to do this is to examine your core skills and how you can transfer these skills to other types of work. Take some time to think about what it is you really like to do. What are you really good at? What special talents do you have? What do you do better than most people you work with? Once you've assessed your core skills, think about how they can be used in other types of work.

Margaret's brother-in-law Bruce is a good example of how you can use your previous skills and experience to get started in a new employment situation in a small town. He increased the diversity of his already-diverse research-lab machining skills when he relocated to a rural community.

The crowds and smog in L.A. were bothering me and I thought, why am I putting up with all this? So I quit my job and moved. Things didn't take off professionally in my new location as quickly as I hoped. So I put together a proposal to work for my former employer in L.A. for one or two weeks a month. Bouncing back and forth has worked fine. I am free to pursue project work here and I have the backbone income from my L.A. job.

—Elaine S.

Drawing on Old Skills to Launch a New Venture	Bruce used to work as a technician / machinist at a university research and development lab. When he and his wife Janet moved to a very small town four and a half hours away, he opened his own business, Round Valley Farm Machinery Repair. The name is misleading. Since he's the only skilled machinist in town, he has been called upon to rebuild the oven box for a turn-of-the-century stove, build a conveyer system for the inside of a container truck, make custom parts for sophisticated machinery, repair old cars, and do wrought-iron work. He also builds new steam engines and restores antique gasoline engines. The most obvious skill transferable from his old job is his experience as a machinist. Perhaps not so obvious is the creative problem-solving experience he gained from working with a research and development group. This has helped him tackle jobs that required many uncommon machining, manufacturing, and prototyping skills.

You Can Make It Happen

Doing something that relatively few have done before can be overwhelming, especially when you want to move beyond the this-sure-is-fun-to-dream-about stage. Rest assured, you're not alone in your quest for an advantageous workstyle and living situation. The alternative workstyles discussed in this chapter have already been tried by many. Not only are they gaining acceptance, they are becoming the norm.

If you are currently working for a company that models itself after something out of a Dickens novel, change may not be easy. You may have to stretch your own imagination and that of your employer too. However, there are organizations out there to help you and an increasing number of success stories to which to point.

Imagine your ideal way of earning a living. What type of work would you like to do? On what kind of schedule? Let yourself dream. In the process we'll lead you through later, you'll draw on your dreams to delineate exactly what you want. To get started, ask yourself these specific questions: Do you want to work for a small local business or for the local plant of a large corporation? Does starting your own business or buying a franchise sound appealing? Would you like to work at home as an independent consultant, work with clients in other locations, travel frequently or infrequently? Are there possibilities in your field of arranging to work at a satellite office or to telecommute from home? What about working on-site on an interim basis and returning home between projects? You can explore these options in any combination.

For now, mull over the possibilities; take long walks; discuss your thoughts with your partner or friends. What would you do if you could take total control of your work life? Current studies say that the typical worker can now expect to have seven careers in a lifetime. But this doesn't mean you have to be a pawn in someone else's bottom-line maneuvers. What do *you* want? It may be that moving to a small town is the perfect way to launch the career of which you've always dreamed.

Wanting It All

Is it possible to find rewarding work that pays decently, uses your skills and talents, and is located in some beautiful small town somewhere in the United States? For many people, we believe it is. Whether you are simply looking for better employment opportunities or are on a quest to find the right balance between work and play, living in a small town can offer new possibilities. The more open you are to alternatives, the more choices you will have.

Of course, employment isn't the only factor in your decision. For a few people, a substantive change would be welcome but moving to a small town just won't cut it. There may be some limiting factors about your current employment or living situation that cannot bend. If this is your case, you may want to consider small cities. The best small cities have a lot of the characteristics you'll find in small towns. The next chapter explores this option.

Small Cities:
A Workable Compromise?

If you just can't see yourself in a small town, consider a small city. It might meet your needs in ways that a small town simply cannot. You might be tied to cities because of job restrictions or special education or medical needs. Perhaps you are a neonatal intensive care nurse and want to continue to work in that capacity. Or you have a child who is a concert-level cellist in a youth symphony. Or your medical care is only available at a few, urban medical centers.

You might also feel that a city is the only place for you for social, cultural, or ethnic reasons. Perhaps you are a single female with a strong passion for opera hoping to meet a man with similar interests. Or you have a strong ethnic identity and want to live where there are many people of the same heritage. If you've been living in New York City, a quaint town in the rural midwest may not offer enough diversity and action.

There are any number of reasons why you might feel tied to a city. But it doesn't necessarily have to be a large metropolis. Some small cities offer many of the advantages of a small town with few of the disadvantages of a large city. Throughout most of this book we focus on small towns. And there's no doubt that many small towns offer more than they used to. But small towns are small for a reason; they don't try to be all things to all people. If your needs, whether professional or personal, require the larger environment of a city yet you desire the community feel of a small town, a small city may be the answer.

Two Ways to Think About Small Cities	**1. Small Cities as a Good Final Destination:**
	    Small cities, at their best, can offer a very good compromise between urban and small-town life. Many offer a wide variety of cultural and economic activities with a lot of the advantages of a small town.
	2. Small Cities as a Good Transition Step to a Small Town:
	    Small cities are good places from which to look for the small town of your dreams. You can pick a small city in the region you desire, and use it as a base from which to build your local network and eventually find your perfect small town.

This chapter explores the different types of small cities. It looks at the elements that make up their character and discusses what makes some more livable than others. As with small towns, finding the right small city for you depends on your particular needs and wants. A small city might be the best of all worlds for you or the worst possible compromise. This chapter will help you explore the small-city option.

Just What Is a Small City?

To someone who grew up in a town with a population of a hundred, Boise is going to seem like a major metropolitan area. From the opposite perspective, to a person who grew up in Manhattan, Boise is going to seem like a small town. Throughout this chapter, though we use the term small city, keep in mind that the term is relative. The ultimate definition of a small town or small city will depend entirely on your own perspective.

Not only does the size of small cities vary tremendously, so does their look, feel, and style. It's important to look closely at what surrounds a place; a small city in a major metropolitan area is going to be vastly different from one in the middle of farm fields. A small city of 120,000 that adjoins a major city of 3 million is going to feel much more like that major city than its rural counterpart. Some small cities are distinguishable from adjoining cities. Some are not. Some are floating in a sea of suburbs; others are surrounded by vast wilderness. And some are a blip on the horizon amid miles of farms and fields. Don't rely on population statistics alone.

> It's physically beautiful. You can see the sky without having to look up all the time. The lifestyle is much better. Everyone is so nice! We were so paranoid that the first night we got here, our neighbors invited us for Chinese food and we kept wondering, why are they doing this? What do they want? In New York, no one would have done this. We never knew our neighbors at all there.
>
> – Leigh P.

| Boise, Idaho | 1990 population: | **125,738** |
| Berkeley, California | 1990 population: | **102,724** |

Population Statistics Aren't Enough

Based on population alone, you might suspect that Boise and Berkeley are similar. Berkeley, however, is but one city embedded among many others within the nation's fourth-largest metropolitan region, while Boise stands on its own in the high desert of the Columbia River plateau. Boise's winter is cold. Berkeley has a Mediterranean climate. Berkeley is a very liberal university town, while Boise is a more conservative community with a strong resource-based economy. Berkeley perches on a gentle slope overlooking San Francisco Bay. Boise looks out over the Rocky Mountains. You can study classical northern Ethiopian folkdance in Berkeley. You can buy any type of logging or ranching equipment in Boise. And so on.

Population statistics alone tell you little about a place. You have to ask what kind of population is in a community. You have to ask what type of surroundings the populace lives in. In short, you have to ask about more than just size.

There are as many types of small cities as small towns, but they are a little easier to classify. Small cities tend to fall into three general categories. Let's take a closer look.

Wanted: A small city that is just a stone's throw from the center of a big city. A place that has plenty of urban stimulation and activity, yet also has its own distinct neighborhoods and sense of community.

Small Cities Within Metropolitan Areas. At one end of the continuum are the small cities that make up larger metropolitan centers. Some have their own distinct downtown areas, others are indistinguishable from their neighbor cities, and others yet take the form of an endless strip. At first glance, it's often difficult to see these cities as anything more than extensions of the dominant city in their area. Up close, evidence of their unique characteristics becomes more apparent. One might have a particularly nice-looking downtown area, older residential neighborhoods, a well-planned park, a certain ethnic mix, or such a focal point as a town auditorium.

Increasingly, it's becoming difficult for small, close-in cities to maintain their individual look and feel. Population pressures, high turnover of residents, poorly controlled growth and development, and other factors erode their distinctiveness. It's also difficult for small cities to be tranquil islands when surrounded by raging urban seas. They often suffer from the same problems as their larger counterparts; crowded freeways, drugs, and crime don't stop at some imaginary border or the city limits.

Some small cities in large urban areas are, however, taking extraordinary steps to create and maintain a sense of community. The individual characteristics of this type of small city vary widely. Finding one that fits you requires research and exploration in the same way that finding the right small town does.

> Of the 248.7 million people in the United States, in 1990, 52.9 million or 21 percent lived in one of the nation's five largest urban areas.
>
> —1990 U. S. Census

Wanted: A small city with a lively downtown, good restaurants, great schools, thriving culture, caring people, and excellent schools, and that is less than one hour from a major city.

Small Cities on the Fringes of Metropolitan Areas. There are some small cities and large towns on the far fringes of urban centers that can offer the best of all worlds. Some are less than an hour from a big city (on a good commute day). They provide reliable public transportation to the metropolitan center, but are far enough away to have small-town character. They have an independent economic base that supports a healthy percentage of local wage earners. They have a strong group of caring residents who are actively participating in the town's affairs and in creating a community.

The small cities differ from suburbs because they have distinct downtown areas and plenty of local merchants and businesses. Their neighborhoods vary in look and age. They aren't bedroom communities where everyone commutes into the big city, casting a silence of daily abandonment over their neighborhoods. People come and go throughout the day. Some have a junior or private college, a small hospital, a large senior center, a sports arena, or another unique feature that draws people in and helps foster a lively interchange throughout the day.

Small-City Personality Quiz

Small cities near metropolitan areas vary widely and may be undergoing rapid change. Here is a quiz to use when determining the depth and strength of a small city's sense of place.

1. Is the housing a mix of
     a) single family dwellings, duplexes, and smaller apartment complexes?
     b) condos and townhouses that all look alike?
     c) high-rise apartment buildings and iron-barred smaller complexes?

2. Are the neighborhoods
     a) mainly older and established or stable?
     b) mostly new, planned communities?
     c) fragmented or physically torn apart?

3. Are the businesses
     a) mostly locally owned, family run?
     b) mainly franchise chains?
     c) boarded up?

4. Is the downtown
     a) a distinct area with thriving shops and restaurants?
     b) indistinguishable from other streets?
     c) run down, with abandoned storefronts?

5. Does the growth and development involve
     a) a little bit of remodeling and construction?
     b) constant construction and new developments?
     c) major demolition, with few signs of reconstruction?

6. On a weekday during the day, does it have
     a) healthy activity, people interacting, kids playing?
     b) nothing but the sound of freeway traffic?
     c) illegal activity, drug deals, robberies?

You've probably already figured out that the "a" answers indicate a healthy sense of place. The "b" answers indicate signs of a commuter city or suburban-style bedroom community. The "c" answers represent serious trouble signs. If most of your answers fall into the "a" category, the place shows promise. However, don't forget to look as well at the elements that form your own definition of a good place to live.

We lived in metropolitan-orbit small cities—all close to San Francisco—for years. Some had more personality than others. During the time we lived in them, however, we saw them change rapidly. The boundaries grew fuzzy as urban problems seeped beyond city limits and into surrounding areas. But more than external forces are at work.

We saw this trend over and over: Housing prices go up, the long-time residents move out, and younger, double-income residents move in. The new residents have long commutes into the big city, rarely see their neighbors, and have limited time for community activities. Crime goes up because there are so few people around in the daytime. Smaller, family-run businesses can't make a go of it because of the increasing rents and property taxes, so they fold and the larger franchises move in or the storefronts remain closed. This downward spiral and erosion of a sense of place is in large part what motivated us to look for a home base outside of a metropolitan area.

The next category is for those of you who are interested in exploring small cities far from the metropolitan centers of this country.

Wanted: A beautiful city with a strong sense of community and family, free of gang wars, riots, and smog; with good schools, inexpensive property, and a feeling of serenity.

Small Cities Miles Away from Metropolitan Areas. At the other end of the continuum is the city that sits virtually alone, surrounded by miles of farms or undeveloped territory. A number of small cities in less populated states fit this category: Helena, Montana; Pendleton, Oregon; Flagstaff, Arizona. Each has a character shaped by its economic base, geographic surroundings, and historical roots.

The farther a small city is from the center of an urban area, the more likely it is to have its own personality. These "stand-alone" small cities vary widely in their style and tone. There are those that have little ethnic diversity and others that are considerably diverse. Some offer little on a cultural level while others are cultural oases amid great natural beauty. One small city might proudly retain the look of a well-preserved, turn-of-the-century town; another might be reeling from uncontrolled growth and a slew of fast-food restaurants.

A small city in the country will tend to be heavily influenced by its surroundings. For example, a rural city in a farm belt will have fairgrounds, a farm auction center, and used tractor dealerships as well as banks, stock brokerages, and fancy restaurants. It serves as both an agricultural resource and a business center for people living miles around it. Main Street may be a mix of farm machinery repair shops, antique stores, and designer clothing boutiques. This is a different kind of diversity than you'll find in a metropolitan small city.

Think about these factors when exploring small cities outside major metropolitan areas:

Evaluating "Stand-Alone" Small Cities

- Why did a city grow there?
- What are its historical roots?
- Is it still tied strongly to these roots?
- Is it in the midst of a transition?
- How fast is it changing?
- Is its growth and development controlled?
- Is it supporting a withering industry?
- Is it actively encouraging new industries?
- Does it show signs of economic stress?
- Is there a regular influx of visitors?
- Is there a diversity of people?
- Is there a diversity of activities?
- Are there overt signs of intolerance?
- Are there indications of open-mindedness?
- Are there signs of a strong community?
- Are there signs of a fractured community?
- Is it strongly influenced by certain groups, defined by religion, ethnicity, age?
- Is it civic minded?

Later in your search process you'll delve more deeply into researching the pros and cons of a place. Don't forget that someone else's pros may be your cons. One person might be thinking duck hunting, whereas the next person is thinking bird watching—but all the Visitors Bureau said was "lots of wildlife, particularly birds."

One last note. Stand-alone small cities are often less plagued by the problems of larger urban areas. Their urban problems are usually smaller in magnitude and more manageable because they are not intensified by the spill-over of similar problems in surrounding areas. However, certain problems are inherent in all cities, small and large, simply because of their size, turnover, and infrastructure. No matter what small city you find, be realistic about the negative aspects of it being an urban environment. The good news is that you will probably find it easier to influence the direction of a smaller city than a larger one. You won't have to shout quite so loudly.

The Economics of Small Cities

In addition to size and surroundings, there is another factor that has a major influence on the character of a small city: its economic and industrial base. Depending on the diversity of a small city's economy and the strength of its industries, it can be a great place to move or a disaster. When times are good, employment opportunities and general acceptance of newcomers tend to be good. When times are hard, many places—small or large—tend to turn inward. For example, if you as a newcomer want to find a local job in a small city that is suffering from a recession, expect to have to work a little harder. When the times get tough, there is always a tendency to hire an old buddy from high school or a second cousin. If you as a newcomer have developed local contacts already, or if you have specific skills that cannot be found elsewhere, you will have a better chance of getting hired.

Evaluating the Economic Side of a Small City	Look closely at what drives the financial side of any small city you consider. Many can be found that have diverse economic bases. A small-city economy may be a mix of traditional agricultural, industrial, and natural-resource sectors combined with an evolving service, software, high tech, or publishing sector. As you start to consider specific small cities, ask these questions:

- Does it have a one-industry local economy?
- Does it have a diverse set of industries?
- Is it encouraging new industry? If so, what types?
- Does it have an economic sector that draws visitors, due to tourism, a college, or special annual events?
- Does it serve a local region only?
- What is its rate of unemployment?
- What is its new-business growth rate?
- What is its rate of business turnover?

The economic character of a small city can determine your employment opportunities. It also affects the city's growth, willingness to accept newcomers, and social and cultural characteristics. A small city that has a steady influx of visitors every year will have a noticeably different feel than a place that lacks the ebb and flow of different types of people. A small city with a college or with lots of tourist activity will generally have a greater selection of cultural events, restaurants, and stores, for example. It may also have the disadvantages of crowds of tourists during certain times of the year and inadequately controlled growth. While a small rural farming city that has practically no influx of new people is unlikely to offer a wide selection of ethnic restaurants and cultural activities, it might have the advantage of a solid, stable populace and well-planned growth. Yes, there are always trade-offs, but there are also exceptions to every rule, so don't expect to predict which trade-offs a small city of particular size and even location might require, before investigating. Chapter 8 will guide you in collecting the data that will help you draw useful conclusions.

Is a Small City Thriving, Striving or Barely Surviving

Here are some questions to help you explore whether a small city is on a healthy growth path or a rocky one.

- Is it on the upswing?
- Is it on the verge of taking an economic nosedive?
- Does it have well-laid growth plans?
- Are they progressing smoothly?
- Is the zoning consistent and well-planned?
- Is the zoning haphazard?
- What are the regulatory controls and how effective are they?
- Are city and county development funds close to running out or bountiful?
- Are there half-finished projects standing idle?
- How active are community members in planning and development issues?

Some small cities have made tremendous strides in revitalizing their downtown areas. They are actively stimulating their economies and cleaning up their environments. Other cities look like the wrecking crew has come and gone, with no cleanup crew in sight. The most difficult to gauge are those that seem okay but are actually wavering on the brink of a fall.

Finding a Small City That Feels Like Your Kind of Town

What makes a small city truly appealing? We've talked about size, location, proximity to urban areas, and economic base. These all have a lot to do with the character of a small city, but there's more. There's that certain something that gives a place, no matter what its size, a special feel. It is difficult to define and impossible to measure, but it must be present: It is a sense of community. Knowing how to recognize a healthy community is crucial if you are looking for a place that feels like home.

The best small cities have what many small towns have: people who come together, who help and appreciate each other, who share their lives. They have a heart and soul. They have a center. Small cities with a true sense of community will show all the signs of people who care and who are involved in shaping their growth and development. In short, these small cities are expanded versions of their small-town counterparts.

Elements of a Community-Oriented Small City	Here are some things to look for:
	• a healthy downtown business
	• popular gathering places
	• people of different backgrounds interacting
	• kids biking to school
	• safe parks
	• well-lit streets
	• well-kept neighborhoods
	• lots of local businesses
	• good public transportation
	• a clean environment
	• well-planned development and growth
	• friendly people

Using This Book to Find Your Ideal Small City

There are many choices on the continuum from small cities that are in large metropolitan areas to those that are in remote rural areas. Later, when you research far beyond your first impressions, you'll check such quantitative information as crime rates, school test scores, and rates of new business development to determine which way a small city is heading. As with finding a small town, it's critical that the place *feels* right as well. This is particularly true with cities because their size makes it harder to assess the true state of their economic and social health.

As you work through the search process in this book, simply substitute the words "small city" for "small town." The only difference you'll experience is during the research phase, which will be easier because you'll find more information available about American cities than small towns.

The next chapter is an overview of the search process. It will give you the big picture of how you'll go about finding the best town for you.

CHAPTER 4
How You'll Find
Your Kind of Town:
An Overview

This book is designed to help you find the small community that best suits both your lifestyle and employment needs. In this chapter, we introduce and explain the process that evolved as we closed in on our own hometown. As our search progressed, and as we learned more about the successful searches of others, we came to see that some approaches seemed to succeed almost without effort and others couldn't be made to work no matter how hard anyone tried. In this chapter we lay the general groundwork for a successful search and the choice of a small town.

We also introduce you to the seven rules that kept our search focused and effective. Actually they are more like guidelines than rules. (The only one we think should be followed in an ironclad fashion is Rule 7.) You'll find that all these rules make intuitive good sense and are easy to follow.

Along with rules we provide safeguards, to steer you away from choosing the wrong small town. They will help you adjust to the inevitable changes of mind, both little and large, that will occur during your search. They will also assist you in reaching and maintaining consensus with your loved ones. And we'll explain a technique we developed for making sure that you, and your loved ones, identify and secure the special requirements on which you just aren't willing to compromise.

We also go over what you need to supply in order to make a successful search. Some money will be required; some time will be required. The amounts vary from person to person, or family to family. However, the most essential requirement is free: it's an open mind.

Yours Is the Only Perspective That Matters

About fifteen years ago a rather obscure band called The Tubes, best known for their fetching rendition of "Don't Touch Me There," had a minor hit song entitled "What Do You Want from Life?" The latter song anticipated the rise of Yuppie consumerism. It ended with the words ". . . and a baby's arm holding an apple." A friend of Eric's at the time thought those closing lines were an allusion. The baby's arm was meant to represent a snake and the apple was the apple offered to Eve.

What You See Depends
on Where You Stand

Observer A sees this

while observer B sees this

and observer C sees this

A   B

C

You and I know that this is an elephant because we see the whole animal depicted. But what about an observer from position A, B, or C? If A described the animal to C, would they be able to figure out they were looking at the same animal?

The friend was a psych major. She saw symbolism in everything. Eric was an English major and thought those closing lines were written about the disgustingly cute little porcelain figurines that his grandmother spent an hour a day dusting.

The point is that no two people see anything even remotely the same way. The question of what you want from life has an answer that is unique to you. This is especially true when you ask yourself in what type of place you really want to live. Choosing a living environment is just too important to be a one-size-fits-all process.

Beware of the resources with "The Best Places to Live" in the title. Their best places are for some hypothetical average person with average needs, based on the author's biases and a battery of statistical data. Unlike these generic resources, the process in this book leads you to a unique list of suitable small towns that fit the caption

"THE BEST PLACES FOR
(insert your name here)
TO LIVE"

The Worksheet Process

The simple, practical, step-by-step process in this book is built around five worksheets that help you assess where you live now, your employment and quality-of-life needs, your search requirements, and your shortlist of towns. A large part of the initial process involves defining exactly what you want to end up with. Once you arrive at your definition of an ideal living environment and employment situation, you use the search worksheets to filter through hard, then soft data to identify a shortlist of towns that best match your ideal.

The worksheets are a starting point. They are designed to be copied, marked up, and organized in a binder. You may want to enlarge or customize the worksheets to fit your unique needs. For example, if you prefer a more free-form style, you may want to transfer the categories and headings of the worksheets into a journal with blank pages.

Moving Only Changes the Pollen, It Doesn't Cure the Allergy

My Kind of Town is not a miracle book for those seeking to solve personal problems by moving away from them. It will lead you along an orderly and simple path to clarify what you want from your living environment, so you can move *to* a better quality of life. It is not going to help those who seek only to move away *from* the problems of their

The Process of Finding
Your Kind of Town

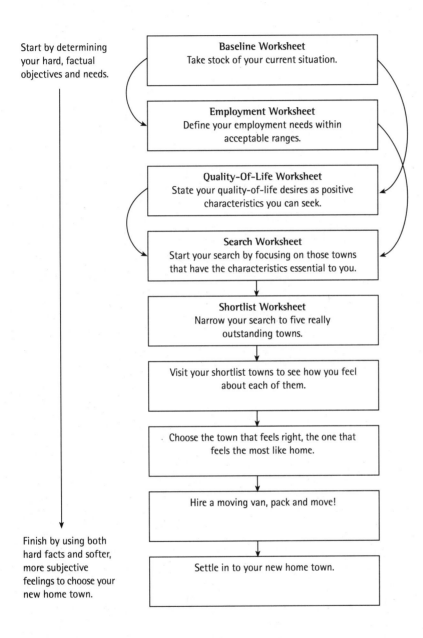

Start by determining your hard, factual objectives and needs.

Baseline Worksheet
Take stock of your current situation.

Employment Worksheet
Define your employment needs within acceptable ranges.

Quality-Of-Life Worksheet
State your quality-of-life desires as positive characteristics you can seek.

Search Worksheet
Start your search by focusing on those towns that have the characteristics essential to you.

Shortlist Worksheet
Narrow your search to five really outstanding towns.

Visit your shortlist towns to see how you feel about each of them.

Choose the town that feels right, the one that feels the most like home.

Hire a moving van, pack and move!

Settle in to your new home town.

Finish by using both hard facts and softer, more subjective feelings to choose your new home town.

This is a flowchart of the search process. We've simplified it for this illustration, but all the big pieces are here.

current living environment, since the same person will be unloading the moving van in Xenia, Ohio, as loaded it in Baltimore, Maryland.

Admittedly, this can be a fine line. You will ultimately have to judge for yourself how much of your dissatisfaction stems from the factors found in your current environment and how much is an inescapable portion of your traveling gear, no matter where you go. We address this issue by structuring the search process so that you define, prioritize, seek, and ultimately choose a small town based on the positive elements you wish to find, rather than the negative elements you wish to leave behind. This structure will feel comfortable and natural to a person wishing to move to something.

The Hard-to-Soft Approach to Research

You will begin by culling the most tangible, factual information first. You will conclude by choosing a small town based on the feelings in your gut and your heart. This hard-information to soft-information approach provides the framework for your search.

The answer to the question "What defines a great place to live?" is actually quite simple: A great place to live is one that gives you all the warm feelings of being at home. That became the starting point in our own search. We outlined the steps that were necessary to eventually find ourselves in a place that gave us those feelings.

It didn't take long to realize that those warm feelings grew in the soil of harder factual information. For example, it's hard to feel at home in a place with a high rate of violent crime. Such crime is regularly measured, so it is easy to rule out those places that have a high rate of violent crime per thousand residents. However, one piece of favorable statistical data cannot make you feel safe in and of itself.

A real feeling of safety and security demands more. Is the local police department highly visible? Are transients dealt with fairly and effectively? Does the local district attorney's office seem to function well? Taken together, many individual pieces of information form the foundation upon which a feeling of safety and security is built.

Some information is more tangible than others. For example, weather and climate represent one of the hardest forms of information. If you are seeking snowy winters and long, hot, dry summers, you can locate a place with these conditions in a climate reference book. These seasonal conditions have been accurately measured and mapped by climatologists and meteorologists. They definitely exist in some places and definitely do not exist in others. Climate reference books can tell

The Hard-to-Soft Research Technique

Hard **Information** **is**	**Soft** **Information** **is**
Measurable	Unmeasurable
Quantitative	Qualitative
Tangible	Abstract
Objective	Subjective
Factual	Instinctive
Statistical	Emotional

Some examples are:	Some examples are:
average temperatures	pleasant weather
population figures	uncrowded feeling
test scores	good learning environment
crime rate statistics	safe feeling

One useful way to view information is on a continuum from hard to soft. Facts and statistics are hard; instincts and feelings are softer and more subjective. Information at all points on the continuum is valid. The search process is designed so that you first find towns that satisfy all of your hard requirements, then move on to qualitative factors, and finally choose a town on the basis of softer information. Considering all types of information, from hard to soft, makes your conclusion reliable.

you what to expect as well as ranges of heat, humidity, and precipitation, number of days below freezing, and a thousand other measures. The data are not subject to much interpretation. You will never enjoy deep-powder skiing in central Mississippi or mild winters in Montana.

By contrast, the quality of schools represents a softer form of information. Yes, the quality of schools can be measured—but by which yardstick? Test scores for any U. S. school district are readily available. But do test scores tell you all you need to know about school quality, or do you need to look beyond the numbers? Is a good school system one with an excellent sports program, one that offers progressive and special programs, or one that emphasizes discipline and the three Rs? (These, of course, are judgments that only you can make.) School-quality information is unlike weather and climate data. It is softer, less tangible, and demands a more subjective, personalized appraisal than does factual data about climates: it is qualitative, midway on the hard-to-soft continuum.

The final category of information is your own feelings. They can't be measured. They are often difficult to define precisely. They change. They are not always rational. (And they don't need to be.) Feelings matter every bit as much as every other form of information you'll use in your research. A small town may have wonderful statistics and dynamite data to offer, but if you don't have a good feeling about the place, you won't be happy there.

Moving from hard information to soft evolved into a very successful research technique for us. If you consider the less variable factors first, you will be able to narrow your list of potential regions and small towns quickly. You will then be free to focus on the softer aspects, give qualitative information its due weight, and also weigh in your feelings about each of your shortlist small towns.

Seven Rules for a Successful Search

These seven rules will help make your search successful.

Rule 1: *Seek a positive trait instead of avoiding a negative one.*

Rule 2: *Allow enough time.*

Rule 3: *Feelings are as important as facts.*

Rule 4: *Be open-minded and flexible.*

Rule 5: *Be inclusive and build consensus.*

Rule 6: *Change your mind whenever you need to.*

Rule 7: *Rules are made to be broken.*

How much will it eat?

Can we train it to clean the leaves out of our rain gutters each fall?

How long is it?

How much does it weigh?

Is it a good house pet?

Is it good with kids?

OK, how much fertilizer?

What will it do if it decides it doesn't like your new necktie?

How old will it live to be?

Will it be lonely if its the only one of its kind?

How tall is it?

Here's the elephant again. You can ask many questions about the elephant, some with hard, quantifiable answers, others with more subjective ones. If you are going to spend any time with an elephant, you need answers to both types of questions.

If one or two rules don't seem to work for you, invoke Rule 7, or if you want to include more, add them. The entire framework here is designed to be flexible so that it will work for you, no matter what your needs happen to be.

Rule 1: *Seek a positive trait instead of avoiding a negative one.*
It is easier to seek one elephant in the jungle than it is to search the entire jungle to prove there are no tigers. For one thing, you can stop looking as soon as you find the first elephant. For another, it's much more pleasant to focus on seeking something positive than to avoid something negative. It will also be a better use of time. Complaining and whining about the negative factors in your life can drain a lot of energy, and you'll find that it is easier to form consensus around a positive goal.

We made this rule the first for a reason; we think it is the most important. If you are looking for a better, more positive life, you are more likely to be successful if you seek specific positive traits instead of avoiding vague negatives.

Rule 2: *Allow enough time.* Choosing a new place to live is a big decision. An extra few weeks to make certain of your decision is a small delay that could save you from a large mistake. You'll need time to figure out what type of town you want to move to. You'll need time for research and to be certain that you and your loved ones have reached a good, workable consensus. You'll need time to ponder and change your mind. You'll need time to visit a few small towns. And you'll need time to choose one.

How much time? If you are single, have a readily portable work situation, and already have a pretty solid definition of your ideal small town, you may be able to start packing in three months. If you have a family, widely varying ideas of what you want from a living environment, and multiple work situations that must also be moved, it is not unreasonable to allow six to twelve months for the process, or even longer. Allow yourself time for changes of mind and adjustments. This is a major decision; don't rush it.

Rule 3: *Feelings are as important as facts.* Because feelings are difficult to measure, we tend to discount them relative to hard facts. Try not to. In this book, we encourage you to give them equal weight. By first rigorously researching and satisfying your hard factual requirements, you are freed to choose a small town with your heart—because your finalist small towns already will have satisfied the requirements of your head.

Rule 4: *Be open-minded and flexible.* Beware of the possibility of passing up an excellent but unexpected option simply because it's unexpected. Remember, serendipity visits those with open eyes and an open mind.

It is possible to find the right small town in a hurry, if you must do so. It is also possible to find the right small town on a very thin budget. But it will be hard to find the right small town without an open mind. Here's why. In your mind's eye, you probably have some picture of the type of small town that appeals to you. That's good. What happens, though, when you find a small town that differs from the picture in your mind's eye but suits you even better? An open mind accepts it as a better choice than originally expected. A closed mind rejects it simply because it differs.

Rule 5: *Be inclusive and build consensus.* If you are planning to move with others, we strongly suggest you include them to the greatest extent possible throughout the search and decision process. This includes children. Listen to the needs of others and respect them. Make your move a winning situation for everybody. Later in this chapter, we talk about the importance of the mind merge technique throughout your search process.

This rule is included for one reason—to strongly encourage you to build consensus among all those with whom you will be relocating to a small town. The more consensus you build early in your search, the smoother the whole process will be.

Rule 6: *Change your mind whenever you need to.* In upcoming chapters you will spend time thinking about many elements of your life that you might not have considered in such depth before. At the start of your search for a new town you may draw some initial conclusions that will change after some research, further reflection, the persuasion of your loved ones, or an argument or two. Some conclusions may change quite a bit. Allow for this. Better to change your mind than to pick a small town based on beliefs you no longer hold.

Rule 7: *Rules are made to be broken.* Rules? Schmules! It has to work for *you*. That's all that really matters. If we suggest a technique or method that doesn't work for you, use another that does.

Finding a town that satisfies your unique needs may require a unique type of search. We encourage you to customize use of the process we present. What if employment is not an issue in your case? Disregard the portions that deal with employment. What if you already know which town you'll be moving to? Take advantage of the portions that have to do with moving and settling in. Bend, modify, reorder, or otherwise change our process in any way you think will make it work better for you.

Safeguards to Keep You on Target

The search process has several safeguards built in, points at which you can stop, review your progress, and double-check that you're on the right track:

The Reality Check. A reality check is a designated opportunity to change your mind without feeling fickle or guilty. When you delve deeply into defining your ideal living environment you may be surprised at how much your views and desires not only will change during the process, as you acquire a more in-depth knowledge of what small towns have to offer, but how much your views will have changed over the last five or ten years, without your even realizing it. This was certainly true for us. Margaret had become less of an urbanite. Eric had become a little more of a social animal.

At key points in the process we will remind you that it's time for a reality check, a simple step in which you review your progress up to that point, then ask yourself some fundamental questions. You can't do too many reality checks, but you can certainly do too few.

The Mind Merge. A mind merge is a means to check whether you and your loved ones are headed in the same general direction. Note, this is not necessarily the same thing as being in perfect agreement. A mind merge is a chance for all participants to speak their minds and move toward consensus. Everyone in your group will be doing a lot of soul searching during the process of choosing a small town. All will be sure to change their views on certain subjects several times over. That is expected and healthy. The mind merge safeguard is designed to bring everyone together to share their latest thoughts and ideas at critical points throughout the process. (*Star Trek* fans will remember something similar: When Spock did mind melds he would put his hands on somebody else's head, read the person's mind, and then go into a coma for the next five minutes of the show. We call ours by a different name, since it normally does not result in a coma for the participants.)

As with reality checks, you probably can't do too many mind merges. With too few, if you move to a small town that falls seriously short of a loved one's needs or desires, the chances of successfully settling into your new hometown will be greatly reduced.

The Must-Haves. A must-have is a factor that you feel absolutely must be present in any small town in order for the town even to be considered. When you're working with a group, it's easy to lose sight of the relative importance that you attach to various factors. Things that matter a great deal are sometimes overlooked. Things that are not really important end up being treated as if they were. The must-haves safeguard is meant to prevent this.

In Chapters 5 and 6, you'll decide what elements and characteristics you wish to look for in a small town. You'll then prioritize these, giving several of them the top status of must-have. (Your must-haves might change as you go through several reality checks. That's normal.)

When we began to define our ideal place to live, we quickly realized that our definitions were about as wide apart as the sides of the Grand Canyon. We wondered if there existed any *one* place that could meet our differing needs. Was there a small town that could accommodate Eric's reclusive yearnings for wilderness and Margaret's sporadic yet powerful cravings for urban stimulus? If not, was there a good compromise? Defining a series of priorities and ranges helped us arrive at several options. We recognized that each of us had must-haves. We also realized that it worked much better to define our respective needs as ranges of acceptability rather than as absolutes. For example, the issue of having a movie house that played foreign films changed to one of having acceptable access to good movies. The issue of living four hours from a city became one of acceptable population density in a certain geographic region. This was a turning point in our search for a small town.	**Building Bridges**

What if two people's must-haves seem to be in direct conflict? In the first place, don't be so sure that they are. If one of you can't live without access to a good college library but the other is sick of college towns, explore living outside of a rural college town. You'll feel miles away from the college scene, even though you might be within a short drive of it. Or check out towns with satellite colleges that offer long-distance, electronic access to classes and library services at the main campus.

In cases of conflict, your research will have to be a little more rigorous. Just be persistent. In the rare instance where satisfaction is not possible, some compromise is inevitable. Thinking of your needs in terms of ranges, staying open minded, and working together to find a solution can produce great results. One couple we know had a major conflict to overcome when he wanted to live in the Pacific Northwest but she couldn't stand incessant rain. Neither particularly cared for the desert topography of eastern Oregon and Washington. They both preferred to be close to the ocean. Through research and a bit of luck, they discovered the idiosyncratic nature of microclimates. Even within the rainiest regions, there were localized areas that had substantially lower rainfall and much more sun than their surroundings.

Together, the couple that disagreed on climate was able to find a compromise that worked for both of them. This degree of success is not always possible and you may have to consider compromising beyond your acceptable range. If this is the case, you'll need to weigh the pros and cons of staying in your current living environment versus moving to a place that is lacking all or part of one of your must-haves. Don't forget that things change. A place that currently fails one of your must-have tests might eventually pass it.

Making Your Search Successful

This book is more than just a passive read. It offers a process, guidelines, and information that will make your search for a better living environment effective and efficient. It doesn't offer any instant or magic answers. The only way to ensure you'll find your kind of town is to take an active role in its pursuit. Closing your eyes and pointing to a spot on a globe, throwing darts at a map, or following the suggestions of friends and family will likely put you miles away from your ideal location. In an exasperated moment early in our search we actually got out the darts. Had we relocated where the darts landed, we would now be living next to a hazardous waste clean-up site rather than snow-covered mountains and clear lakes.

There will be some expenses associated with the search. You will need to do a fair amount of photocopying. You will want to write letters and make long distance phone calls, for example, to various public agencies, local chambers of commerce, real estate brokers, school districts, and potential employers. There will be some reference books that you won't find in your local library and will probably wish to purchase. You will probably want to buy some supplies with which to set up a filing system for the information you will uncover during the course of your research.

The biggest expense will be for travel to the small towns that eventually make it onto your shortlist. This may not be possible for some people, but if at all possible we *strongly* suggest that you spend some time in the two or three towns at the top of your list, before finally choosing one. You can research most of the factual and some of the qualitative information about a small town from a distance. You can even cultivate a circle of friends over the phone. But you will have to spend some time walking around on Main Street and talking to people in order to be sure the town feels right for you. There really is no other way.

The next section provides a solid, step-by-step process, but it is up to you to make it work. You now know how the process is designed for you. You know what is required of you to ensure that your search is a success. You have seven guidelines that will help your search go smoothly, and you know that key safeguards will help you stay on target during this process. It's time to dive in and start.

two

Making the
Right Move

CHAPTER 5

The Baseline Worksheet:
Taking Stock of
Where You Live Now

A baseline provides a starting point. Whether your present situation is workable and merely in need of repair or you are committed to great geographic change, you will be able to make a more informed decision about your future if you have a working inventory of your present situation. That's what the Baseline Worksheet is designed to provide. The worksheet provides the "before" photograph. The "after" photograph will be you in your new town.

First you get to vent a little, then you get to dream. Be sure to work *in pencil* on a photocopy of the blank Baseline Worksheet. You'll be erasing, changing, and adding to each of your worksheets almost up until the moment you return from visiting each of your shortlist towns. Make it easy for yourself when you decide to change your mind.

○ **Step 1: List the Negatives**

You probably wouldn't have picked up this book if you hadn't been at least a little bit dissatisfied with your present living situation. Doubtless, there are some things that you'd change if you could. Now is the time to put your dissatisfaction down on paper.

Look at your personal situation. What are the things you dislike about your life that are a function of where you live? What are the disagreeable aspects of your life that could be altered by a change of address? Write them down. A few short words is all you need. Your entries might look like this:

- *Fred's commute is too long.*
- *The schools are deteriorating.*
- *It's not safe at night.*
- *Housing is too expensive here.*
- *It's growing too fast.*
- *Fred's job isn't challenging.*
- *Too little time for kids.*
- *Too far from skiing, camping.*

- *The smog is horrible.*
- *Too little time for fun.*
- *Deb's job requires too much overtime.*

The Baseline Worksheet

Step 1   List the negatives:

Too far from (outdoor fun (hiking, skiing))   HOME

Too many (cars/peeps)

Too little time for fun

(Crime) increasing

(Weather) crappy

(Housing) too expensive

Don't fit in community

Too few acceptable bike rtes

Few convenient good rest/(bakeries/health food)

No (Town center) (greant)

(Commute) probably req'd

Step 2   List the positives:

Perfect distance from (relatives)

Convenient shopping

(M/ auto)

Highway convenient

(Salaries) good

Job (Network) here

(Internet access), cheap, good, cov't

(Friends fairly close by.)

Very short (commute).

Set up for non-car travel, (Pedestrian-friendly)

Aesthetically (appealing)

Something we (LIKE)

Step 3   List the ideals:

Home office possible   ready to conv'n land,

Pvt yard w/ (trails) land,

- Veg garden req'g no maint
- Compost pile
  - workshop

Workout room

2-Car garage + bsmt

porch/deck — screened

No (skeeters)

Good bike routes.

Leash laws in all local towns.

Hi-spd, cheap (Internet access.)

Close to (X-C skiing/hiking/MTB,)

(Mt views), (lake)

(Liberal)

Health food store/(Food Coop) + Shops,

Good, creative (rest + bakeries)

Convenient Shopping modern products

Convenient (hiway)

Both to cut back to (30 hr/wk.)

Access to (Univ)

Step 4   Highlight core topics:

Get a felt-tipped marker and highlight the subject of each phrase in Steps 1, 2, and 3 above.

Good (race of peeps) w/ similar interests

Not overrun w/ (tourists)

Good bike shop.

Steady, not booming, (growth.)

Perfect distance from (relatives)

Meaningful (work)

Flexibility

Time to work out regularly

Flexible hours

Write down everything that you can think of right off the bat. Then set it aside. Plan to come back to Step 1 a little later and see if there are other things you want to add. There probably will be a few.

○ **Mind Merge**

When you give everybody who is contemplating a move with you a chance to add their input every step of the way, you change the process from one of an individual making a decision for others to one of building consensus among everybody. The consensus route may be harder at first, but it will result in a more successful search.

Try these techniques early on: get all participants together and agree on how you want to gather everyone's input. You might decide to hold formal weekly meetings or a series of informal dinner discussions. To avoid putting each other on the spot, we found it worked best to bring up a topic in the morning, let each other stew on it for the day, then discuss it that evening.

Remember Rule 5:
Be inclusive and build consensus. **Your loved ones may have some gripes that you haven't thought to add. Let them give their input.**

○ **Step 2: List the Positives**

In Step 2, list all of the things that you like about the place you now live. This one may be a little harder. After all, as we said before, you probably wouldn't be reading this if you weren't dissatisfied with your present situation. Still though, there must be some things that are right about your present living environment.

Rule 1 gets its first workout here: *Seek a positive trait instead of avoiding a negative one.* As you think of these positives, write them down. Just a few words will do fine. All you need is enough so that you'll be able to look at the completed worksheet later on and remember what you were thinking when you wrote each positive trait down in the first place. Here are some examples:

- *The climate's good here.*
- *Stu's piano teacher is excellent.*
- *Wong's Chinese restaurant.*
- *I like our church.*
- *There's good live music here.*
- *Deb likes her job.*
- *Our friends, family are here.*
- *Fred's salary is good.*

You get the idea. Write down all the positives you can think of now, set the worksheet aside for a while, then come back to it a little later and see if you've got any other entries to add.

○ **Step 3: Fill in the Ideals**

In Step 1 and Step 2 you wrote down elements of your present living situation, both positives and negatives. What about all of the elements that are not present in your current life, the ones you'd really like to have?

You'll like this step. This is where you get to define your ideal world. In Step 3, write down all the things that you'd like to have in the perfect living situation. Don't limit yourself. List as many as you can think of.

You may have been no closer to a horse than the time you went to the video store and rented a John Wayne western, but if you've always wanted to live someplace where you could have horses and go riding from your back door, write it down here. This is where you get to dream about your ideal home and work life. Anything is fair game. Remember, these elements will be the nucleus around which you define the type of small town you are searching for.

Here are a few examples to start you thinking:

- *Deb would like room for horses.*
- *Four real seasons would be nice.*
- *A private yard.*
- *We should be able to walk to work.*
- *There should be lots of old trees.*
- *We want a friendly neighborhood.*
- *It should be small enough that we matter.*
- *It would be great to be near fishing.*
- *We'd like a nice old Victorian house.*
- *Deb wants to cut back to part-time work.*
- *Fred would like a more interesting job.*
- *Steady but not booming growth rate.*
- *Easy for Grandma Ellen to get around.*

For a moment there you probably had a brief vision of what your ideal town might look like. It looked pretty good, didn't it? Leave lots of room for dreaming as you start to define the type of town you think you want to live in. You'll be able to make some of those dreams come true.

An Imagination Exercise	Someone once said, it's difficult to see the picture if you're inside the frame. If you're having trouble seeing beyond your current life, try this: Start at the beginning of the alphabet and think of all the words beginning with an A that might describe your ideal living situation. For example, apple orchards, alps, alfalfa fields, adventures, agreeable, antiques, appealing, arid, artistic, athletic, awesome. (List nouns, adjectives, verbs, whatever.) Now, go on to "b" words, then "c" words, and so on. As the words flow, let your dream grow. Play this game alone or with several people. You can write the words down, or simply use this exercise as a way to get your imagination going.

O **Mind Merge**

Some of your loved ones may have gripes, or positive comments to add, or dreams of doing things that they cannot do where you live now. Everyone wins when you find a small town that makes a few of those dreams come true—and loses when you don't. Exploring your small-town options could be complicated by a loved one's foot-dragging if they feel left out of the process. So as you complete your Baseline Worksheet, work toward consensus by actively soliciting a list of ideals from *all* of your loved ones. Make sure, from the very moment you start to ponder the idea of a small-town move, that everybody sees the change as one that could directly benefit them. Share your ideas. Establishing an "everybody wins" atmosphere from the beginning bodes well for an "everybody wins" conclusion.

O **Step 4: Highlight the Core Topics**

....

We wanted a better place to raise kids, where the cost of living was lower so Cindy wouldn't have to work.

—Bob M.

This is a stepping-stone to the next chapter. It'll take a few minutes and a felt-tipped highlighter. On your Baseline Worksheet, highlight the core topic of every entry you made in Steps 1, 2, and 3 above. The filled-out Baseline Worksheet provides examples.

In the next chapter, you'll use these core topics to define the exact characteristics you'll seek in a small town. Before going on to the next chapter, however, step back and take a look at your completed Baseline Worksheet.

A Snapshot of Your Life

We didn't want to compete with the designer-label mentality of the suburbs.

—Cindy M.

Your completed Baseline Worksheet indicates what is and isn't working in your life at this moment. And perhaps more important, you've also indicated what is missing in your life that you want.

This is valuable information. Right there, on one sheet of paper, is a condensed version of your life today. What patterns appear in it? First, are there a lot of entries that concern one topic, employment or

The Baseline Worksheet

Taking Stock of Where You Live Now

Step 1 List the negatives:

Fred's commute is too long.

The schools are deteriorating.

It's not safe at night.

Housing is too expensive here.

It's growing too fast.

Fred's job isn't challenging.

The smog is horrible.

Too far from skiing, camping.

Too little time for kids.

Too little time for fun.

Deb's job requires too much overtime.

Step 2 List the positives:

The climate's good here.

Stu's piano teacher is excellent.

Wong's Chinese restaurant.

I like our church.

There's good live music here.

Deb likes her job.

Our friends, family are here.

Fred's salary is good.

Step 3 List the ideals:

Deb would like room for horses.

Four real seasons would be nice.

A private yard.

We should be able to walk to work.

There should be lots of old trees.

We want a friendly neighborhood.

It should be small enough that

we matter.

It would be great to be near fishing.

We'd like a nice old Victorian house.

Deb wants to cut back to part time.

Fred would like a more interesting job.

Steady but not booming growth rate.

Easy for Grandma Ellen to get

around.

Step 4 Highlight core topics:

Get a felt-tipped marker and highlight the subject of each phrase in Steps 1, 2, and 3 above.

schools or crime, for instance? If so, you will want to pay close attention to that issue in your search. Now, take a look at the balance of items under Steps 1, 2, and 3. Are there a lot more negatives than positives? If so, displeasure with your present situation suggests you have energy to change. What if there are just a few negatives and a lot of positives? Maybe things aren't all that bad where you are now after all.

Compare your ideals to your positives and to your negatives. What do you see? Are there a lot of things missing from your life? Do you get really fired up by the possibility of pursuing those ideals? Also, do you see any patterns among your ideals themselves? Do they tend to deal with certain topics, such as work or leisure-time activities? Such signposts suggest productive directions for your search.

Our Own Negatives, Positives, and Ideals

These were the entries on our own Baseline Worksheet. Some of these will apply to many other people, while others are particular to us.

Negatives:

It is too crowded here now.

The cost of living is absurd.

It is too violent and hostile.

The schools here are getting worse.

Too little time for family and friends.

Too much time wasted sitting in traffic.

Impossible to buy a decent house.

Fear of crime.

Not part of a real community.

Positives:

Our family and friends are here.

Margaret has a good job.

A lot of great music.

The weather here is good.

Easy to see foreign films and experimental theater.

Great restaurants and coffee shops.

Ideals:

We want to be near mountains and water.

We want to be part of a real community.

A place one to two hours from a city with airline service.

Time to work on creative projects.

Good schools.
Friendly people.
Fewer hours working and commuting.
More family time.
Four real seasons would be nice.

How You'll Use Your Baseline Worksheet

The completed worksheet will form the nucleus of your search for a small town, as a prioritized list of goals. Again, we invoke Rule 1: Seek a positive trait instead of avoiding a negative one. We are not the type of people who never ever say a cross word to anybody and have smiley-face bumper stickers on our cars. Our reason for steering you away from negative issues is more pragmatic. It is more efficient to search for a positive than it is to avoid a negative. After all, you're searching for a small town because you want a better place to live, right? So why not concentrate on finding a place that has positive elements, rather than avoiding the negatives? The difference may seem semantic, but more than that, it's the difference between searching out one elephant in the jungle and searching the entire jungle to prove there are no tigers. It makes success possible.

So why did we have you list all the negatives? Because they are probably the biggest reason you are considering small towns in the first place. And they'll come in handy, though not in their present form. In the next chapter, we'll show you how to take all the negatives you listed and turn them into positives. This will make your search for a small town both more efficient and more enjoyable.

CHAPTER 6

The Employment Worksheet:
What Do You
Want from Work?

If Employment
Is Not an Issue...

If you are retired, or have a career that can move anywhere, or do not need to think about employment at this point, skip this Employment Worksheet chapter and continue directly on to Chapter 7.

Defining Your Ideal Employment Situation

Here is a summary of the three steps you'll take to complete the Employment Worksheets. By the end of this chapter, you will have a customized vision of your perfect small-town work situation.

First, you'll assess what you like and don't like about your current employment situation. You've already accomplished much of this in the previous chapter. You'll take the negatives, positives, and ideals that you have already listed on your Baseline Worksheet, and rephrase each one to be a positive attractive characteristic. Each characteristic will be listed on a separate Employment Worksheet. Then you'll add additional characteristics to this stack as needed.

The second step involves an in-depth examination of each attractive characteristic. You'll establish a range of acceptable options for fulfilling that characteristic. There will be plenty of examples to help you through this stage.

The third step will be to rate each characteristic. There's no room for fence-sitting, so this step might take some time. To sort your priorities and determine how much you're willing to compromise, you'll start by selecting the characteristics that you absolutely cannot do without. These will be your "must-haves." You'll finish by identifying the characteristics that would be "nice to have."

After you've completed these steps on your Employment Worksheets, you'll go through a similar process for your quality-of-life requirements in the next chapter.

Using Employment Worksheets to Define What You Want

Of the thorny questions that arise when thinking about moving to a small town, many concern employment: How am I going to make a living?

> The really efficient laborer will be found not to crowd his day with work, but will saunter to his task surrounded by a wide halo of ease and leisure.
>
> —Thoreau, *Journal*
> (March 31, 1841)

Can I continue in my current career? Do I want to make a major job change? These issues loom in front of us, sometimes blocking our way. They can seem like obstacles too large to overcome. Don't let them dissuade you. Once you fully explore your options, you'll very likely discover that you have more choices than you realized at first.

	Some Typical
There aren't any jobs in my field.	**Concerns About**
There aren't any jobs similar to the one I have now.	**Small-Town**
There aren't any jobs even remotely like the one I have now.	**Employment**
There are some good opportunities, but the pay seems low.	
I'm worried about job security/benefits/pension.	
I don't know how to find out about jobs in small towns.	
My skills aren't transferable.	
My license(s) or credential(s) aren't transferable.	
There aren't any employment opportunities for my spouse.	
I want to start a business but don't know where to start.	
I have entrepreneurial skills but lack funds.	
I have an established business, but it may not do well in a small town.	
I'd like to move my business to a small town but can't afford to.	
I'd like to buy a franchise but don't know how to evaluate it.	
I want to start a new career but need retraining.	
I'm ready for a change, but I can't figure out what kind of change.	

There are many alternatives in climate, geography, or the size of a community. For most people, however, there are not quite so many choices when it comes to making a living. A Los Angeles mass transit worker cannot become a small-town lumber mill equipment operator over-night. The most sought after skills of an ad-agency account executive in Manhattan may not be in such high demand in small-town Nebraska. There are often relicensing requirements when a school teacher, attorney, or chiropractor seeks employment in a new state. These are the sorts of obstacles that you might face, to one degree or another, as you consider moving to a small town. With some creativity, however, there are ways to clear these hurdles.

At the top of the Employment Worksheet you'll notice this:

Before you start this Worksheet, repeat Rule 4 out loud:
Be open-minded and flexible.

It seems to be an almost mathematical rule that, for us and for the other émigrés to small towns we know, an inch of flexibility buys a yard of extra options. Nowhere is this more true than in the area of employment. An open mind and a willingness to be adaptable can make the hurdles a lot lower than you might have initially imagined.

<table>
<tr><td>

**A Study
in Adaptability
and Flexibility**

</td><td>

Page and Steve moved from a major metropolitan area to rural Arkansas. They bought a farm with the intent of raising chickens for Arkansas's booming chicken industry. Soon after they moved, however, the chicken deal fell through. They could have returned to the city, but they had fallen in love with their thirty acres of rolling hills, house, barn, pond, and woods. *At first, we tried to find work that drew on our past experience. Steve had done landscaping and construction. I had done writing and photography. We looked everywhere, but there were so few jobs. The economy was really depressed and we hardly knew anyone. Steve got certified as an asbestos worker and did asbestos removal. I applied for all kinds of work. We tried raising some crops. We went to Memphis to work for a few months. Then I got a job at the University of Arkansas, about an hour away from our farm, doing student counseling. Steve decided to finish his college degree and he got a part-time job working for the agricultural extension. Two years later, I lost my job when the federal grant money was cut. But by this time we knew a lot of people and the university hired me to teach several English and art classes. Meanwhile, Steve graduated and has been offered a great job in North Carolina, so we're going to move to a small town there. Who knows what's going to come next.*
—Page C.

</td></tr>
</table>

There are many ways of earning a living. Some jobs just get you by. Others are important stepping-stones in a career. Today, the nature of employment is undergoing some serious changes. Staying in one job, or in one company, is a rarity. It's more common to have a series of different jobs and even vastly different careers, throughout your life. Increasingly, people are approaching employment in stages rather than as one long continuum. We work hard for awhile, then stop or cut back while raising children or to go back to school or to pursue a personal goal. These days, you might find yourself earning a living in ways you never dreamed as a youngster.

....
**It's easier to make a
career change if you
already have an
established network.**

—Elaine S.

When we first moved to a small town, Margaret had quit her job to have another baby and to pursue some creative projects, and Eric had a steady shipping job for a large corporation. We were not dependent on the local economy for the bulk of our income. After a year, however, Eric was diagnosed with asthma and could no longer work on ships. We embarked on an intense employment analysis to determine our options. Would we have to move? Would one or both of us have to do a daily, long commute to the city? Were there any local opportunities at all? Could we start our own business?

Margaret began to explore long-distance electronic contracting and telecommuting alternatives in video and multimedia production. She examined the types of work she could do from a home studio, with a minimum of travel. She decided to focus on interactive multimedia design and production. Much of the work could be done on computer and transmitted via fax and modem. However, renewing her old professional network and finding clients located close by took some time. She spent six months commuting into the city a couple of times a week to establish contacts and build a new network. She also traveled to other, larger cities, sensing that there might be greater opportunities farther afield. After awhile the contracts began to trickle in, and soon there was a steady stream.

Meanwhile, Eric launched the writing career he had always dreamed of pursuing. He took a local part-time job to help make ends meet and continued to search for work that better matched his skills and interests. After several months, a part-time opening came up at a publishing company that had recently moved to town and Eric was hired. Throughout his months of job searching, Eric stayed in touch with lots of local people through volunteer work. This proved to be an effective way to find out about opportunities early on. It also provided an excellent support system. Now, Eric has a good part-time job and is able to pursue his writing goals as well. He is also working with Margaret in her multimedia business. A dream that seemed years away has come true: we are able to earn a living doing the work we like in a beautiful, healthy environment. It hasn't always been a smooth road, but fortunately the bumps have had an uncanny way of moving us forward instead of holding us back.

Now it's time to photocopy the Employment Worksheet from the Blank Worksheets appendix, if you haven't already done so. Figure that you will need at least fifteen copies of the worksheet per breadwinner. Maybe more.

O   **Step 5: Develop Attractive Employment Characteristics**
Retrieve the Baseline Worksheet that you filled out in the last chapter and put a check mark by every item that has to do with work, employment, or income in any way. This includes items that may not be directly related to the job itself. Commute length, a boss who's a member of the human race, overtime requirements, and interesting work are all fair

The Employment Worksheet

Before you start this Worksheet, repeat Rule 4 out loud:
Be open-minded and flexible.

Step 5 One attractive employment characteristic of my kind of town is:

_____

_____

Step 6 Describe the range of acceptable options for this attractive employment characteristic:
One end of the range is: The other end of the range is:

_____   _____

_____   _____

_____   _____

_____   _____

_____   _____

Step 7 Prioritize this employment characteristic:

A must-have _____

Very desirable _____

A good idea _____

Might be nice _____

Step 8 Describe research resources for this employment characteristic:

_____

_____

_____

_____

Completing the Employment Worksheet

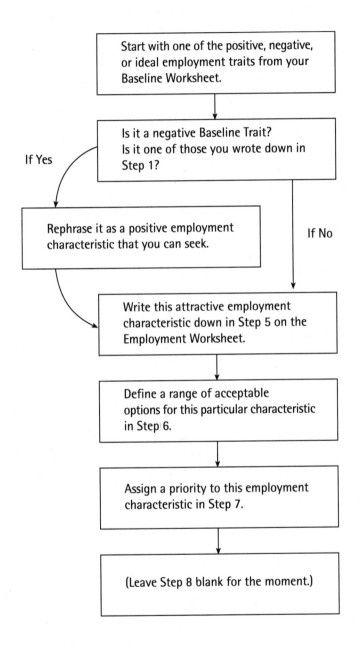

Start with one of the positive, negative, or ideal employment traits from your Baseline Worksheet.

Is it a negative Baseline Trait?
Is it one of those you wrote down in Step 1?

If Yes

If No

Rephrase it as a positive employment characteristic that you can seek.

Write this attractive employment characteristic down in Step 5 on the Employment Worksheet.

Define a range of acceptable options for this particular characteristic in Step 6.

Assign a priority to this employment characteristic in Step 7.

(Leave Step 8 blank for the moment.)

topics. Express each of these as a positive characteristic on a separate Employment Worksheet, at Step 5.

Remember to turn each negative statement from Step 1 into a positive when you enter it on its own Employment Worksheet. For example, "Deb's job requires too much overtime" becomes a characteristic to pursue when stated "Deb can work part time." In addition to the advantages we've already mentioned, positive statements allow greater precision. The more precise your portrayal at this stage, the clearer your choice of a town will eventually be.

State It in Positive Terms	Here are some examples of negative statements and how they can be transformed into positive characteristics.
	
	The negative statement
	    Fred's **commute**'s too long
	becomes the positive characteristic
	    Fred can have a **short commute.**
	
	The negative statement
	    Deb's job requires **too much overtime**
	becomes the positive statement
	    Deb can **work fewer hours.**
	
	The negative statement
	    Fred's **job is very boring**
	becomes the positive statement
	    Fred can have **a challenging job.**

○ **Also for Step 5: Fill In the Gaps**

If you made seven check marks you should have seven Employment Worksheets so far. Each participant may want to generate a set. (You'll combine them later.)

Next, leaf through these Employment Worksheets and think hard: What's missing? Are there some holes in your portrait? Are there more aspects of work life that you want to consider before you choose a new town? If so, now is the time to fill them in. You might feel tempted to omit traits that seem farfetched or impossible to attain, but stay open to them. If you limit or censure yourself at this point, you'll never know whether what you really want is out there.

Take some time to ponder the sample questions below. There are no right or wrong answers to these, only sincere ones. The minute one of the questions spurs you to say "Hey! It sure would be great if . . . ," grab a blank Employment Worksheet and complete Step 5. Also browse through the Resource Appendix at the back of this book, to further explore the range of your options.

Employment Questions to Ponder

Here are some questions to help you fill gaps in your stack of Employment Worksheets. The goal is to have every good element you can envision about a small-town work situation on an Employment Worksheet.

To define what you might really want to do, ask yourself:
- What do I like/dislike about the field I'm in?
- What do I like/dislike about my present job?
- What job/career have I always wanted to have?
- What are my established experience and skills?
- What are my undeveloped skills and talents?
- What other jobs have I had?
- What other jobs could I do?

A great part of the process to follow builds on the employment data you establish here. Be sure to make use of Rule 2: *Allow enough time.*

When Mike F., an anesthesiologist, left Los Angeles, he left his medical career behind. *When I walked out of that hospital I took a leave of absence, but I think I never intended to go back. The reason I went into medicine wasn't there anymore. I was sick of the hassles.* After he moved to a small town, Mike decided to try something really different: tax preparation. *I've always enjoyed doing my own taxes, and after we moved I needed to learn some new things, so I took a class. It turned out that anyone taking the class could take an exam and get licensed, so I decided to give it a try. It's a lot of fun. There's a lot of helping people through stressful situations, but there aren't any life and death emergencies in taxes.*

Trading One Taxing Profession for Another

To consider something completely new, ask yourself:
- What is my dream career?
- Can moving to a small town help me launch a new career?
- How are my job skills transferable?
- What amount of risk am I willing to take?
- What retraining steps do I need to consider?
- How fast a career transition do I want to make?
- What is the best strategy for me?
- Do I know of anyone who has made similar changes?

| **From Weekend Retreat to Weekday Home** | Ed and Anita spent a lot of weekends driving back and forth from the city to their favorite small town. Ed had his own consulting business in the city, but as he got to know people in the small town he started to take on some clients there. One thing led to another and he was hired as a full-time financial officer by one of his clients in the small town. *We thought we wouldn't move out of the city until we reached retirement age, but then we realized there was no reason not to move now.* Anita, an insurance investment consultant with clients in the city, is steadily finding more clients closer to home. She now drives into the city only once or twice a week. |

To explore options in your present situation, ask yourself:

- Do I want to continue in my present job?
- What commute range is acceptable to me?
- How portable is my type of work?
- Does my work lend itself to working from home, or from a satellite office?
- Is my company open to new ways of working, such as tele-commuting, flexible hours, or long-distance employment? (Even if it's not, yet, could I make a strong case for any of them?)
- Does my current employer have a branch, outlet, or division near a small town that would appeal to me?
- Can I switch from staff employment to a contract business to increase my flexibility?
- Could I stay in my present job during a transition period until I find or create a local job?

| **From Missiles to Muffins** | Mac and Amy quit their highly skilled jobs for a defense engineering company and moved to a small town with the dream of starting a bed-and-breakfast inn. From their previous jobs they brought with them solid knowledge of management, accounting, contracting, marketing, and other business procedures. Their transferable business skills helped them launch a successful, professional bed-and-breakfast inn. *We had this plan that one of us would work out of the house and the other would run the B&B. We've done a lot of oddball things to try and find that other real job. That first winter, I worked as a bartender and Amy waitressed. Then I worked for awhile, helping a local manufacturer set up a factory. Then Amy ran a small bookkeeping business. Now, Amy's working as a software engineer for a company about an hour away. She works out of a home office three days a week and commutes there the other two days. It's working out well.* |

To accommodate two careers, ask:

- What does my partner like about his/her career?
- Do my partner and I have more or less the same definition of what constitutes an ideal small-town work situation?
- Are we both open to exploring new career opportunities?
- Are we interested in working together, such as by starting a business or buying an existing one?
- Do I, or does my partner, want to stop working for awhile?

Liz and Bill both worked as sales and marketing professionals for a computer software company. They quit their jobs to move to a small town. *Initially, we thought we'd buy an established retail business. Our first goal was to move to a small community. Our second goal was to find a business that would support us. We were open to just about any type of business.* And open-minded they certainly proved to be. Liz and Bill eventually started their own business breeding emus (a kinder, gentler member of the ostrich family).

Trading Mega Bytes for Mega Birds

To put money issues in perspective, ask:

- How much will I need to earn?
- How much will my spouse need to earn?
- What are the financial needs of my dependents?
- Would it bother me to earn less money than I do now?
- How much of my present income goes to the trappings of my career (clothes or entertainment, for instance) that I might not have to spend if I live and work in a small town?
- What is my comfort level regarding financial risk?
- Do I need a backup resource, such as fallback job skills, savings, or a leave of absence from my current employment?
- How much of a safety net do I need to establish for myself, or for my family?

The last set of questions, regarding your comfort level with financial risk, is worth giving some extra consideration. Risk is a part of change. The act of moving to a small town, especially if you are making a major career change as well, involves risk financially (what if my new employment is a bomb?), socially (what if nobody in the town likes me?), and personally (what if this was all a big mistake and I want to move back to the city?). Knowing your comfort level and planning accordingly will help you through some of the decision-making process to come.

For us, when moving to a small town started to look like a serious possibility, a lot of questions about risk sprang up suddenly. They evoked very different comfort levels. Margaret, who is financially cautious, had never quit a job before without having another one already lined up. She was fearful of quitting her job outright and not having something waiting in the wings. Eric, on the other hand, was more willing to adopt an attitude of "we'll work it out as we go."

We planned for Eric's job to be our primary source of income for the first couple of years after we moved. His job security looked excellent. Meanwhile, Margaret explored the possibility of taking a leave of absence, which would give her the option of returning to her job after a year in case things didn't work out. She found that we were moving too far away for this to be a realistic option. Finally, we determined that Margaret should stay a few more months at her job so we could bolster our savings. All of these steps helped reduce both the risk and the fears we had about making such a big change.

| Reducing Your Risk Anxieties | When you face an unknown, talk about what the worst-case and best-case scenarios might be. This gives a boundary or framework to what's ahead and can help calm your fears. |

- Explore your feelings about risk.
- Discuss your anxieties and fears.
- Talk about your hopes.
- Determine what you have control over.
- Look at what you don't have control over.
- Figure out what factors really push your adrenaline button.
- Determine what you can do to alleviate these specific factors.

Nearly all of our discussions about risk seemed to start with, "What happens if . . . ?" And of course there's no way to really know. It helps to face your fears honestly and to determine what level of risk you can live with. Once you've done this, you can focus on your best-case scenario with greater confidence. As it turned out, we did have to face our worst-case scenario when Eric had to stop working on merchant ships for medical reasons. It was a difficult period and we were thankful for that extra bit of savings we had hoarded before we moved. But even this "worst-case" turn of events turned out for the best.

There are different ways to reduce your employment risk when moving to a small town: extra savings, fall-back jobs, incremental change. Bill and Liz chose a small town close enough to a city so that Liz could find a high-tech sales job until they got their emu ranch off the ground. As it turned out, Liz never had to make that commute. *I thought I'd have to work in the city for a year or two, until our business took off. I was used to traveling a lot, so it would have been okay. But the emu business turned out to be really profitable much quicker than we thought it would, so I didn't have to go to the city.*

Did the long list of questions above add a few new sheets to your stack? We hope it did. If you feel that the elements of your ideal small-town employment situation are not quite complete, you'll need to do two things. First, rather than worry that your portrait isn't filled out to the last detail, remind yourself that it will become more complete as your search process continues. Second, keep a few blank Employment Worksheets on hand. Every time you think of some new aspect of small-town employment that you'd like to find, write it down at Step 5 on a new Employment Worksheet.

○ **Reality Check**

Take a look at your current employment situation with a cool, practical eye. What can change? What can't change? What must change?

○ **Mind Merge**

If you're considering moving with a spouse or partner, the above questions may have also sparked a few lively discussions. Good. That's healthy. You are contemplating a major change in your lives; such a change should not go without discussion. Take this time to double-check each other's thinking. Make certain that you're talking the same language.

○ **Step 6: Describe the Ranges of Acceptable Options**

In this step you put the limits of your flexibility down on paper. For each employment characteristic that you listed at the top of an Employment Worksheet, frame a question. How much of a commute is acceptable? What range of income could you live within? How quickly (or slowly) do you intend to make your career change? This can be a little tricky. After all, how can you be certain of your future needs—income, commute, or career type, for example—especially if you don't know exactly what type of small town you're looking for? Are we asking you to look into a crystal ball?

Yes, in fact we are. But we're guiding you to define what you see there for yourself and then to check it against reality, repeating these steps until the picture you see in the crystal is solid. Step 6 will help you sketch out a rough design of what you want in your future small town. When you rough out acceptable ranges, you define your parameters. Write in pencil. Keep an eraser handy. Stay open-minded.

Thinking in terms of ranges allows a lot of flexibility. For example, you may find that in small towns houses cost less than you thought. This would allow you to lower your minimum income needs. You may find that some small towns have more career opportunities than you thought possible. This might enable you to broaden your range of acceptable types of employment. It may become apparent that there are too few dual career opportunities, that is, for both you and your spouse, in remote small towns. This might mean adjusting your acceptable proximity to a larger town or city. Trust that your employment information will firm up as your search for a small town proceeds.

Okay, let's start. Say for instance that, at Step 5, the first Employment Worksheet in your stack says, "The town's size is big enough to support my air-conditioning business." From looking at your business in its present location, you can probably estimate how many potential customers are necessary to support your business in a new small-town location. Perhaps the air-conditioning industry association has some market data on the minimum-size market that will support a business of your type. Say you determine that you need to be in a small town with a population of 5,000. That establishes one end of a range. Write "population of at least 5,000" at Step 6 in the left column.

How about the other end of the range? You may want to add a buffer in case the economy turns down. So let's say that you are a little more comfortable with a community of 7,500 people. Or you may want an even greater buffer if you are thinking of moving to a small town in a cooler climate. But you don't want to move to a town that's too big, or you'll be likely to run into already established competitors. You'd prefer to be the only air-conditioning business in town. So you decide the high end of your acceptable range is 10,000. Write "population of no more than 10,000" at Step 6, in the right column.

As always, keep an eraser handy. During your research and search steps in the next chapter you may learn that a lot of towns of 10,000 in the hotter climates of the South and Southwest can, in fact, support two air-conditioning businesses. At that point, you could adjust the high end of your range upward.

Here's another example. Let's say you are a graphic artist. You already work at home, and you plan to continue doing so in any small town you move to. Still, you know you will have to be near a midsized city so that you can find clients and go see them relatively easily. But you don't want to be too near. You might want to think in terms of driving time. Living thirty miles from certain midsized cities means it will usually take you no more than forty-five minutes to get into the city. That's close enough, you say. How far is too far? Two hours of driving time? OK. There's the other end of your range.

You may not be able to determine all of your ranges of acceptable options at this point. Some might require a bit of research, or more soul searching. That's okay. Just fill out what you can now. You can fill out the rest as you go through this and the next chapter.

○ Step 7: Prioritize Your Employment Characteristics

Some employment characteristics matter a little, some matter a lot. As your search progresses, you'll want to be sure to give enough attention to the things that matter a lot. The only way to be sure the important things get enough attention is to separate out the less important elements.

The Employment Worksheet gives you four ways to prioritize or rank any characteristic you seek. We've provided a small, even number of choices for a good reason; if you use an odd number, your responses will tend to gravitate toward the fence sitter's middle "maybe" answer. Also, the greater the number of choices, the greater the likelihood that you'll gravitate toward the safety of the middle answers. With a one-to-ten evaluation scale, for example, the four-five-six range is overwhelmingly popular. Having only four choices forces you to take a stand.

Let's define the categories. A "must-have" is something that is vitally important to you. It is something you are absolutely unwilling to compromise on. Everybody has one or two. Some people have more. Your must-haves form the initial filter that will help you eliminate the vast majority of towns out there and quickly get to those that best match your portrait. We suggest that you select no more than five must-haves. This will force you (and the others in your group) to do some really in-depth soul-searching.

"Very desirable" characteristics will help strengthen your personal small-town filter. "A good idea" characteristics will be useful in further narrowing your choices, particularly when you get to your shortlist of possible small towns. "Might be nice" characteristics come in handy when you get down to the final stage, choosing between two or three candidate towns.

....

All you get from fence-sitting is splinters.

—Old Swedish proverb

The Employment Worksheet

Before you start this Worksheet, repeat Rule 4 out loud:
Be open-minded and flexible.

Step 5 One attractive employment characteristic of my kind of town is:

A salary for Fred that lets us keep our lifestyle at about the same level.

Step 6 Describe the range of acceptable options for this attractive employment characteristic:

One end of the range is:	The other end of the range is:
If our small-town cost of living is	*The same salary as Fred makes now,*
25% lower, then Fred's salary could	*or more.*
go down by about that amount.

Step 7 Prioritize this employment characteristic:

A must-have   X

Very desirable

A good idea

Might be nice

Step 8 Describe research resources for this employment characteristic:

First, we need to make up a really accurate family budget. We'll want to check

housing prices very carefully. Fred will have to ask about salary early in his job

interviews. Find out about local tax rates, utility costs, and any other costs of

living before we pick a town.

The Employment Worksheet

Before you start this Worksheet, repeat Rule 4 out loud:
Be open-minded and flexible.

Step 5 One attractive employment characteristic of my kind of town is:

Deb can cut back to part-time.

_____

Step 6 Describe the range of acceptable options for this attractive employment characteristic:

One end of the range is:

As little as half-time, on a flexible

schedule.

The other end of the range is:

No more than 30 hours a week, on

a fixed schedule.

Step 7 Prioritize this employment characteristic:

A must-have _____

Very desirable _____ X _____

A good idea _____

Might be nice _____

Step 8 Describe research resources for this employment characteristic:

_____

_____

_____

_____

The Employment Worksheet

Before you start this Worksheet, repeat Rule 4 out loud:
Be open-minded and flexible.

Step 5 | One attractive employment characteristic of my kind of town is:

We can walk to work.

Step 6 | Describe the range of acceptable options for this attractive employment characteristic:
One end of the range is: | The other end of the range is:

Within a 10 minute walk of work. | *If our walk is more than 25 or 30*

minutes each way, we'll end up

driving, so no more than 20 minutes

on foot.

Step 7 | Prioritize this employment characteristic:

A must-have _____

Very desirable _____

A good idea _____X_____

Might be nice _____

Step 8 | Describe research resources for this employment characteristic:

The Employment Worksheet

Before you start this Worksheet, repeat Rule 4 out loud:
Be open-minded and flexible.

Step 5 | One attractive employment characteristic of my kind of town is:

A loose dress code at work.

Step 6 | Describe the range of acceptable options for this attractive employment characteristic:

One end of the range is:

To be able to wear more comfortable

clothes when the weather is bad,

at least.

The other end of the range is:

A really casual atmosphere where

people dress formally only when they

have an appointment.

Step 7 | Prioritize this employment characteristic:

A must-have _____

Very desirable _____

A good idea _____

Might be nice _____ *X* _____

Step 8 | Describe research resources for this employment characteristic:

As you start checking off priority ratings on your worksheets, sort them into four corresponding stacks. If you're not sure about one or two characteristics, make your best assessment for now. Let each stack sit for a while. A few hours. A day. Even a week. In the back of your mind, you'll probably mull over and reorient a few priorities. Keep in mind Rule 6: *Change your mind whenever you need to.*

When you come back to your four stacks, look through them again. Ask yourself these questions:

- Are you comfortable with the employment must-haves you've chosen?
- Are you being absolutely honest with yourself about what you want and need from employment?
- Are you being flexible?
- Are you being realistic?
- Have you omitted anything critical?
- Have you included your loved ones' considerations?

If you find more than a few worksheets changing stacks after you've taken a second look, you may want to let them sit for a while again. Take a third look. By the third time, you'll probably be much more certain of your priorities.

By precisely and creatively defining the employment situation you seek, you lay the foundation for a happy and fulfilling small-town life. What about Step 8, at the bottom of the worksheet? You don't need to do that yet.

Now for a change of pace. It's time to focus on the quality-of-life characteristics you wish to find in a small town.

CHAPTER 7

The Quality-of-Life Worksheet:
What Do You
Want from Life?

The worksheet in this chapter is a tool to help you identify the quality-of-life elements that are particular to you. If you filled out Employment Worksheets, the Quality-of-Life Worksheets process, though a little different, will be familiar to you. Each one of the worksheets is like a piece of a jigsaw puzzle. As you fill out more and more of them, they may start to look like a lot of puzzle pieces rattling around loose in a box. Don't be discouraged. Hidden in that box of disorganized puzzle pieces is a portrait of the small town you will eventually discover and move to. Soon you'll begin putting the pieces together.

Defining Your Ideal Lifestyle

Before starting the Quality-of-Life Worksheet, repeat Rule 6 to yourself once more in a firm and commanding voice: *Change your mind whenever you need to*. And you should. We changed our minds more than a few times at this point in our search. And so did just about every other person we spoke with. It's inevitable that your thoughts, priorities, and wishes shift over time. Expect it, and allow for it. Remember to write in pencil, and get more erasers before you begin.

Though it's not emblazoned at the top of the worksheet, keep in mind Rule 7, too. *Rules are made to be broken.* If we suggest an action or step that is not right for you or your situation, modify or ignore it. Use what works well for you.

You'll need copies of the Quality-of-Life Worksheet to work with. Photocopy at least a dozen to start with; you may need forty or more before you finish.

O **Step 5: Develop Attractive Quality-of-Life Characteristics**

On the Baseline Worksheet you filled out in Chapter 4, look at each item you did not check off as an employment-related issue when you started the Employment Worksheet. These items have to do with quality-of-life issues. Start with Step 1, the negatives, changing each one into a positive statement and entering it at Step 5 on a Quality-of-Life worksheet.

The Quality-of-Life Worksheet

Before you start this Worksheet, repeat Rule 6 out loud:
Change your mind whenever you need to.

Step 5 One attractive quality-of-life characteristic of my kind of town is:

_____

_____

Step 6 Describe what this quality-of-life characteristic *really* means:

_____

_____

_____

_____

_____

Step 7 Prioritize this quality-of-life characteristic:

A must-have _____

Very desirable _____

A good idea _____

Might be nice _____

Step 8 Describe research resources for this quality-of-life characteristic:

_____

_____

_____

_____

_____

Completing the Quality-Of-Life Worksheet

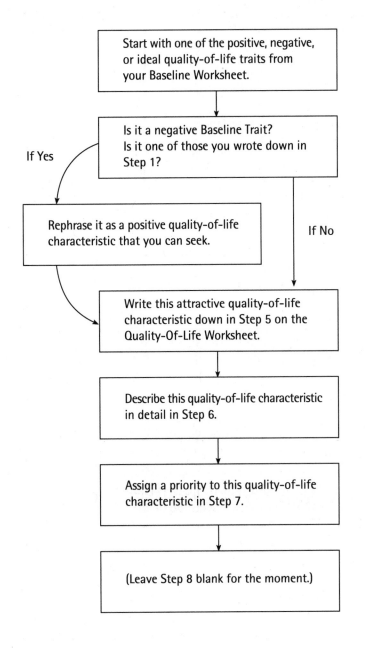

Start with one of the positive, negative, or ideal quality-of-life traits from your Baseline Worksheet.

Is it a negative Baseline Trait? Is it one of those you wrote down in Step 1?

If Yes

Rephrase it as a positive quality-of-life characteristic that you can seek.

If No

Write this attractive quality-of-life characteristic down in Step 5 on the Quality-Of-Life Worksheet.

Describe this quality-of-life characteristic in detail in Step 6.

Assign a priority to this quality-of-life characteristic in Step 7.

(Leave Step 8 blank for the moment.)

Work your way through all the negative quality-of-life aspects of your current living situation that you listed on your Baseline Worksheet.

State It in Positive Terms

Here are some quality-of-life negative statements transformed into positive characteristics.

The negative statement
> The **schools** here are deteriorating

becomes the positive characteristic
> I want a **good, stable school system.**

The negative statement
> It's not **safe at night**

becomes the positive characteristic
> We need a town with a **low crime rate.**

The negative statement
> The **smog** here is horrible

becomes the positive characteristic
> I want to live where the **air is clean and clear.**

The negative statement
> My **hay fever** is really bad here each spring

becomes the positive characteristic
> We need to find a place with **a low pollen count.**

The next group of Quality-of-Life Worksheets, taken from Step 2, the positives on the Baseline Worksheet, will be more straightforward to express. You can enter each of these at Step 5 with few changes. For example, "The climate's good here" becomes a characteristic to pursue when stated "A really good climate." When you finish with the positives, begin a worksheet for each ideal characteristic in the same way.

○ **Also for Step 5: Fill in the Gaps**
Did all the things that matter to you make it onto a Quality-of-Life Worksheet? Since you completed your Baseline Worksheet you may have thought of other things that you'd like to find in a new town. If so, write them in now. If they matter to you, even a little, write them (in positive terms) at Step 5 on their own Quality-of-Life Worksheets.

For example, comfort while roaming the neighborhood on your bike, or relaxing in a hammock with a good book, might not have appeared on your Baseline Worksheet. You could translate them into the following attractive characteristics:

Safe, friendly neighborhoods
Slower pace
Good bike paths
Private garden with shade trees

Don't forget unique personal factors. For example, are there any special health needs that must be accommodated? Do you want to go back to school? Do you want to live close to certain relatives or friends? A single factor, such as finding a town in an area with a low pollen count, can help narrow your search quickly.

We found a number of factors to add as we proceeded. Eric noticed how much more attractive neighborhoods with buried public utilities are. That became something we searched for, and found. Margaret realized that positive aspects of a college town—such as great bookstores, good coffee shops, and stimulating intellectual discussion—could be found in places without colleges. We looked for, and found, a place that met that description.

Day-to-day hassles and lack of time can make it difficult to see past your current situation. After several years in a rigid box, it may be difficult to imagine life in a more fluid bubble.	**A Quality-of-Life Brainstroming Exercise**

Indulge now in a little daydreaming. Shut your eyes and let your mind wander beyond the boundaries of your hectic daily consciousness. Think about your favorite vacations. Ponder childhood memories that bring a smile to your face. What was it about their environments that made you feel good? Which aspects could you duplicate in a small town?

Add as many more Quality-of-Life Worksheets as you feel you need. The way that you personalize your search can be the difference between discovering a good town and a truly great one.

○ **Step 6: Describe What This Quality-of-Life Characteristic Really Means**
So far, you have a stack of paper with an attractive-characteristic statement written at the top of each sheet. As you read these positive statements to yourself, you might have a clear vision of what each one means to you. You could leave it at that, but we suggest that you don't.

Having a detailed description of what each characteristic means to you will sharpen and speed your search later. It is also a critical part of building consensus with the others in your group.

For example, you may have written "The local schools are good" in Step 5. But you haven't spelled out what that means. Is it a heavy emphasis on the three Rs? Lots of funding for alternative education programs? Good sports programs? Adequate special services? Without a clear definition of what "good schools" means to you, you risk being misled during your research by opinions and data that have been built on quite a different definition of "good schools."

Here's another example for those who are moving with others. Two of you might agree that you both want to live somewhere with lots of trees, but for one of you this might mean groves of palms and for the other, a pine forest. It's easy to think you know what the other person has in mind, but assume nothing, especially when you start to define factors in detail. The personal attributes are the most intangible of all; "safe," "lively," "active," and "friendly" are all adjectives that can be interpreted many different ways.

If you try to fill in your descriptions all at once it could drive you nuts. Take your time. You'll need it. Go through each of your Quality-of-Life Worksheets, one by one, and fill in Step 6. The examples here will help you with the process.

You don't have to write pages about each one. Just write enough to clarify in your own mind what you really want. Shoot for twenty words. In most cases you'll end up with fifty. Give examples. Erase and add to your description as what exactly makes a characteristic attractive to you becomes clearer.

How to Describe What a Quality-Of-Life Characteristic _Really_ Means	Just saying _I want a good climate_ isn't enough. Ask yourself questions like these:

Just saying _I want a good climate_ isn't enough.
Ask yourself questions like these:

- What kind of good climate?
- What weather when?
- What type of weather makes me feel great?
- Do I want two, three, or four seasons?
- Do I care how long the seasons are? Or how short?
- What is my hottest acceptable temperature? My lowest?
- What are the minimum and maximum acceptable amounts of rainfall? Snowfall? Wind?
- What about my tornado phobia?

It is important to ask yourself the what, when, where, how, how-much, and how-little questions in order to crystallize your thinking, which will be essential when you start your research. As you evaluate various locales, the specifics that solidify your definition of an ideal small town will be the magnets that will pull you toward the towns that best suit your needs. A little extra effort here will save you a lot of extra work later.

Here's how one family described their idea of "good weather" when they filled out Step 6 of the Quality-of-Life Worksheet:

We definitely want cooler, less humid summers. We'd like an average tempera-ture of about 80 or 85 degrees in the summer, and about 20 to 25 degrees in the winter. Some snow is okay, but preferably only in December, January, and February. Rainfall should be less than 40 inches a year.

Your definition may be quite different, but you should try to put at least this much detail into Step 6 of every Quality-of-Life Worksheet you complete.

○ **Step 7: Prioritize Your Quality-of-Life Characteristics**

Rank each characteristic with a check mark by one priority level on each Quality-of-Life Worksheet. Just like the Employment Worksheet, each sheet provides four choices, enough to prompt your making a judg-ment but without one middlemost choice for easy fence-sitting.

Of the four choices, must-haves are the few critical factors that you absolutely are not willing to do without. They will be the most important determinant in your research and search steps in the next chapters, and you'll use them over and over again. Remember, work in pencil!

Your "very desirable" factors are not quite as critical as your must-haves, but they still substantially define your vision. "A good idea" factors will be useful particularly in narrowing your shortlist of small towns. "Might be nice" factors will come in handy when you get down to the final stage, choosing between two or three similar towns.

Sort your Quality-of-Life Worksheets into four stacks, correspond-ing to the four priorities, and then set them aside. Go into the kitchen. Put on the kettle. Feed the cat. Come back and go through your stacks again. You'll be amazed how much you can change your mind in a few short minutes.

Move the sheets around. Do you have too many must-haves? Too few? Do the priorities feel on target? If not, erase, reprioritize, take

The Quality-of-Life Worksheet

Before you start this Worksheet, repeat Rule 6 out loud:
Change your mind whenever you need to.

Step 5 One attractive quality-of-life characteristic of my kind of town is:

A good school system.

Step 6 Describe what this quality-of-life characteristic *really* means:

A small average class size—25 students or less. There should be computer

training starting in middle school. The district should have a low drop-out rate.

A high percentage should go on to college. The district should rate in the top

20%. Discipline should be firm. No violence in the schools and no more metal

detectors at the entrances!

Step 7 Prioritize this quality-of-life characteristic:

A must-have _____X_____

Very desirable _____

A good idea _____

Might be nice _____

Step 8 Describe research resources for this quality-of-life characteristic:

_____

_____

_____

_____

_____

_____

The Quality-of-Life Worksheet

Before you start this Worksheet, repeat Rule 6 out loud:
Change your mind whenever you need to.

Step 5 One attractive quality-of-life characteristic of my kind of town is:

Clear, clean air.

Step 6 Describe what this quality-of-life characteristic *really* means:

No smog. No smoke. No pollution. And a very low pollen count.

Step 7 Prioritize this quality-of-life characteristic:

A must-have _____

Very desirable _____X_____

A good idea _____

Might be nice _____

Step 8 Describe research resources for this quality-of-life characteristic:

The Quality-of-Life Worksheet

What I Want from Life

Before you start this Worksheet, repeat Rule 6 out loud:
Change your mind whenever you need to.

Step 5 | One attractive quality-of-life characteristic of my kind of town is:

Location reasonably close to family and friends.

Step 6 | Describe what this quality-of-life characteristic *really* means:

It would be nice to be within 500 miles of where we are now. That way we could get

the kids together with their cousins over the holidays.

Step 7 | Prioritize this quality-of-life characteristic:

A must-have _____

Very desirable _____

A good idea _____ X _____

Might be nice _____

Step 8 | Describe research resources for this quality-of-life characteristic:

The Quality-of-Life Worksheet

Before you start this Worksheet, repeat Rule 6 out loud:

Change your mind whenever you need to.

Step 5 One attractive quality-of-life characteristic of my kind of town is:

A movie theatre that plays foreign films.

Step 6 Describe what this quality-of-life characteristic *really* means:

It would be nice to find a theater that plays foreign films fairly regularly.

Not just French films, some good Japanese, German, and Swedish films would

be good.

Step 7 Prioritize this quality-of-life characteristic:

A must-have _____

Very desirable _____

A good idea _____

Might be nice _____ X _____

Step 8 Describe research resources for this quality-of-life characteristic:

another break. Be prepared to change *many* of the check marks you've made over the next few days and weeks. Be patient. Sooner or later you will run out of either changes or eraser.

If you *really* aren't certain how you feel about some of the characteristics, just leave the Step 7 boxes blank. Some of them may be difficult to prioritize, especially if it's been awhile since you've assessed your personal goals and objectives. It won't hold you up if you don't assign every characteristic a priority at this point in the process, so don't feel bad about leaving a few of them unanswered now. Just review them periodically.

○ **Reality Check**

Before you start the next chapter, and with it the research that will ultimately lead you to your ideal small town, it is a good idea to review all your worksheet responses one more time. Try to grasp them as a whole. Ask yourself these questions:

• *Are you being absolutely honest with yourself about what you want?* You may also be thinking about a career change or a relationship change, in conjunction with a move to a small town. If so, build it into the process. Ignoring important pieces of the puzzle will complicate your move tremendously.

• *Are you allowing your thinking to change, or are you holding onto outdated goals and objectives?* Give yourself plenty of time. Think about the big picture. What do you want your life to be? This could be one of those rare moments in life when you get to start with a virtually blank sheet of paper. What is the picture you want to see?

• *Are you comfortable with the priorities you are assigning?* If you are having a hard time prioritizing, you may want to spend more time clarifying your own personal goals. They are what determines the importance of one characteristic when compared to another.

• *Do you feel comfortable with the must-haves you've chosen?* Moving from your current living environment to life in a small community is a major transition. Just the thought of it may provoke soul searching on many levels. Allow yourself the freedom to adjust your priorities— especially your must-haves—as required.

What Is the Big Picture of Your Life?

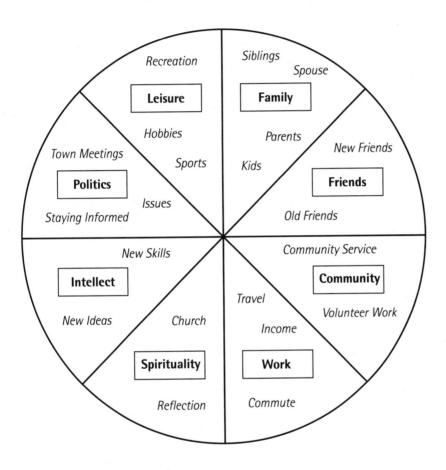

If you are designing a new life in a new town, make sure you include the components you want, in the balance you want.

- *Have you omitted anything?*

Examine how your complete living environment fits the picture you envision. Then go back through the worksheets and make any adjustments you think are necessary.

- *Are you limiting yourself for some reason?*

If there is one regret that most of the émigrés to small towns we've talked with express, it is that they limited their options more than they needed to. Consider the full range of the options you have; examine every component of your life.

O **Step 8: List Your Research Resources**

For every characteristic that you intend to find in a town, you need to know how and where to research it. Step 8 will help you start organizing your resources, and ease into the research process.

First, get out all the Employment and Quality-of-Life Worksheets you've completed so far. Take a close look at each of the employment must-haves you compiled in the last chapter and the quality-of-life must-haves from this chapter. Each sheet contains a positive statement that deals with one topic. For example, your must-haves might include:

Good schools for the kids
A **mild climate** with no snow
Within two hours of a city
A small, lively **college town**
A **good nursing home** for my mother

Without too much thought, a few possible sources of information about each topic probably come to mind. Think in general terms about where you're going to look, who you're going to ask, or what you'll need to find in order to determine whether a town does meet each characteristic.

Tip	This is a good time to scan the Resource Appendix at the back of this book. You may get some ideas about the types of information that are available and the places you could go to find it.

Some of your information resources may prove fruitful and others may not. You may not be able to get a good grasp on the local housing prices until you actually visit a town. Or perhaps you never seem to

For your income needs you might write:

Describe research resources for this employment characteristic:

First, we need to make up a really accurate family budget. We'll want to check housing prices very carefully. Fred will have to ask about salary early in his job interviews. Find out about local tax rates, utility costs, and any other costs of living before we pick a town.

You might approach your school research this way:

Describe research resources for this quality-of-life characteristic:

State department of education for test scores, dropout rates, graduation rates, etc. A teacher's union rep would be able to tell us a lot. Visit the schools with the kids. Talk with the teachers and the students.

Weather or climate issues might be approached in this manner:

Describe research resources for this quality-of-life characteristic:

Get weather data books out of the library. Contact NOAA to see what they have. Talk with the nurseries in each town. Find the closest university agricultural extension branch to get local and regional information.

reach the right person at the local utility company. To a certain extent, that's to be expected. You will probably end up finding, choosing, and moving to a small town without answering every single last research question. At this point, however, think about what's possible, expecting that the resources you develop now will lead you to others.

Two Kinds of Research Resources

Do you notice a pattern in the research resources listed on the sample worksheets? Both "hard" and "soft" information are listed. Hard information is typically numbers, statistics, test scores, or maps. Soft information might be word-of-mouth information from a TV weatherman about a local climate, your own impressions of a school from visiting classes, or suggestions and advice from local people with first-hand knowledge.

Seek both and use both kinds of information. This is very important. We can't emphasize it enough. Everyone seems to know intuitively that hard information is necessary to answer the questions soft information can't. But we all seem to forget that soft information also answers the questions hard information won't touch.

Complete Step 8 by building a research-resource list for the Employment and Quality-of-Life Worksheets that you've filled out. Don't worry if you're stumped on a few worksheets. Some topics will be easy to research, others will take a little more imagination and resourcefulness. You'll be able to fill in the gaps later. Work your way down the ladder of importance from your must-haves to the characteristics you decided might be nice. Draw on your own ideas, refer to the Resource Appendix at the back of this book, talk with friends and colleagues.

You'll probably find that some resources apply to more than one of the characteristics you're researching. The first person to kill two birds with one stone was the first to get consulting fees as an efficiency expert. You might want to make a separate list of general resources that are likely to provide information about multiple characteristics.

If there are still some holes in your research resources, that's OK. There's an adage among sailors: "Every ship leaks a little." A ship with a few leaks can still carry what it's intended to carry. The trick is to be able to tell the difference between the big leaks you must patch and the small ones you might not have to. When one resource doesn't have the information that you want, ask if they know where you might find it.

This list will help you fill in your research resources, Step 8. These are only a start. There are literally thousands of other sources of information beyond those listed here:

Schools:
- The local school board
- The people at the church of your denomination
- The state department of education
- The local teacher's union
- A visit to the schools

Climate:
- The local garden club
- The National Oceanographic and Atmospheric Administration (NOAA)
- The local farmers' or ranchers' associations
- The local radio or TV station's weather broadcaster
- Local nurseries
- The Federal Aviation Agency (FAA)

Local Economies:
- The Chamber of Commerce
- Economics departments at nearby colleges and universities
- State or local professional associations
- The U.S. Census Bureau

Public Safety:
- The local police or sheriff's department
- Local newspapers
- Law schools at nearby colleges and universities
- People on the street

Recreation Opportunities:
- The local sporting goods store
- Editors of the fishing, skiing, or bicycling magazines you read
- The state department of recreation
- Travel agents

Employment Opportunities:
- The state or local Chamber of Commerce
- Local temp-worker firms

- The local employment office
- Local or regional labor union offices
- Local service clubs such as the Lions or Rotary

Specialized Medical Services:
- The nearest teaching hospital
- State or regional health insurance groups
- Associations like the National Cerebral Palsy Association and National Cancer Association
- The American Medical Association (A.M.A.)

Environmental Questions:
- Ducks Unlimited, Bass Masters, and other hunting / fishing groups
- The local Sierra Club chapter or other environmental groups
- The Environmental Protection Agency (E.P.A.)

Cultural Activity:
- The entertainment editor of the nearest newspaper
- Local ethnic associations
- Music, drama, and art departments of nearby colleges and universities

Measures of Proximity to a City:
- A good road map
- The local office of the State Highway Patrol, for information about year-round road conditions
- The regional "puddle-jumper" airlines, for information about the closest scheduled airline service
- The local Chamber of Commerce, for names of businesses in the area that have similar urban-proximity needs

Agricultural Information:
- Farmers', growers', and ranchers' associations
- Pesticide, herbicide, and fertilizer vendors
- Local organic-gardening clubs
- Local nurseries

Where to Now?

This is a turning point. Until now you have been developing a theoretical ideal through the lens of where you are now. You have defined your current work and living situation. You then decided which aspects of your current situation you wish to retain and which you wish to improve. And we'll guess that, if you are at all like us, you have not looked so closely at your own life or lives in a long while. After this chapter, though, the perspective shifts to looking outward at what the world really holds.

By the end of the next chapter, you will have found the region or regions you want to live in. You will have done enough research to have located ten or so small towns that meet your must-have requirements, as well as a good number of your other needs. You will be ready to narrow the field to the few small towns that will be your shortlist finalists. It's time to begin your research.

CHAPTER 8

The Search Worksheet:
Zeroing in on Your
Favorite Towns

By now you have a rough sketch of your ideal small town. You can probably even see a picture of the place in your mind's eye. Are you starting to wonder how you're going to match up this theoretical portrait of perfection with an actual town, in an actual region, in an actual state? Here's how: research.

When you mention *research* to people their reactions tend to fall into two general categories. The vast majority of people run and hide in a dark corner with their fingers in their ears until you stop saying the R word and go away. By now it must be dawning on you that finding your kind of town is going to involve a little research. (Well, maybe more than a little.) If you're like most people, the thought terrifies you. So it's best that we not put this off any longer. *This* is the research chapter.

We have to admit that we are in that small group of people who actually like to do research. Because we do, we know shortcuts. Because we know very well that most people don't like to do research, we've included every shortcut tip, hint, checklist, and suggestion that we could possibly think of.

There's no voodoo here. The techniques are simple. First, the must-haves that you designated in the employment and quality-of-life chapters will be used to eliminate the unacceptable towns right off the bat. Next, you'll use the Employment and Quality-of-Life Worksheets, organized by the four priorities, to guide your research. You'll use your highest-priority needs to narrow the field, then your medium-priority needs to narrow it still more, and so on. By the end of this chapter, you'll be ready to choose a shortlist of small towns, each of which meets most of your hard, factual needs.

The Art of Research

Research can lead you into dark, musty stacks of endless data, or it can open whole new vistas. The following are means of pursuing the data you need in lively, effective ways.

Make Research Fun. Research is more than data. Small towns are made up of a little pavement, a little wood, and maybe some stone, but mostly they are made up of people. So when you research any small community, what you are *really* researching is its people:

- How do they live?
- How do they work?
- How do they run their schools?
- How do they run their communities?

As you research, take time to get to know the people you talk with. Five minutes on the phone shooting the breeze about nothing in particular can sometimes yield spectacular results weeks later when you least expect it. Besides, it's friendly and it can be a lot of fun.

Be Patient and Persistent. The two things you can predict about any research project are first, it will not go as quickly as you'd like, and second, you will have to ask some questions many times before you get adequate answers. In the same way that trucks designed to do heavy work have extremely low gears so they can apply a lot of low-speed power to their wheels over a long period of time, you need to get in gear to do research. Before starting, mentally push in your clutch and drop it into compound low, and maintain a steady foot on the accelerator. Go slowly, so you don't overheat. That way you'll be sure to get to your destination.

Good research is made up of equal parts patience and persistence. The details and results of any research project are unique, but every piece of good research is the culmination of persistence over time.

Patience + Persistence = Good Research

The Basis of Research

Chat. Chat. Chat. Imagine that all the people you talk with during your research have overstuffed Rolodexes on their desks. Each Rolodex is a little gold mine of information. Take time to get to know these people a little. Be pleasant with them. More than once we got a call or a letter from somebody we had talked with saying something like, "I know you didn't ask about this but I thought you might be interested to know that / talk with / see this copy of, etc. . . ." Each of these was like a little gift from heaven. They provided answers to questions we hadn't even thought to ask.

Be Thorough. Find, inspect, and use the little scraps of data about the towns you are considering. Be dogged in the pursuit of the information you need. If there isn't much information out there, that's all the more reason to get ahold of every shred that exists. If your first call or letter to a source doesn't produce the answer you'd hoped for, ask that source to suggest other people you might contact.

Be Inventive. Government agencies aren't the only ones that collect data. Try other sources. The local Chamber of Commerce will have some interesting numbers squirreled away somewhere. The members of the local farming or lumbering association may have some unusually detailed climatic data. As before, be persistent. If your net comes up empty after your first inquiry, ask to be pointed in the right direction, and cast it again. It will almost always be fuller the second time around.

Use Primary Sources. This one is particularly important. A primary information source is one that gives you information straight from the horse's mouth. It may be that the information you seek has never been formally studied. Still, you need that information in order to make your decisions. What do you do? Ask the people who are likely to know firsthand. Ask teachers questions about schools. Ask sheriffs about crime. Briefly explain what you need to know and why. Listen closely to what they tell you. In many cases, it will be the best information you'll get. Use it. Trust it.

Don't Expect Perfection. If you expect your research to be perfect before you make a decision, you'll die with exactly the same street address you have now. The purpose of this book is to help you move to the small town that suits you best. Research is only a step on the way. With every characteristic, there will be a point at which you will have to say to yourself, "I could probably get more information on this subject, but I think I already have enough information to make a good decision." It is possible to pick your perfect small town without having completed 100 percent of your research.

Resist Rushing. If you rush your research, it will make you crazy. State governments can be slow to respond to queries. It can take several calls to reach the one person with a key bit of information. Once you have the information you seek, it can take *you* time to make sense of it in your own mind. And once you have made sense of it, it can take just as long for your family to wrap their brains around the same information. Allow enough time. This is too important a decision to rush.

How much time is enough time? It took us three years—but we didn't have the benefit of a book like this. If we had, it might only have taken us one year. We did everything the hard way at first. That meant we wasted a lot of time. So, how much time should you allow? Three months would be a blinding show of speed. Don't be surprised if it takes you six months. A full year between your first itch to find a small town and the day the moving van arrives may not be unrealistic.

There's one more argument for taking your time; if you have others to consider, the more time you take, the more time you'll have to build consensus. The stronger the consensus, the smoother the transition to your new small town will be.

Be Aware of Your Resources. Researching a small town presents a different set of obstacles than researching larger entities, such as cities or states. States and cities are huge, so there is a compelling reason (and therefore a budget) to study them in depth and detail; thousands of people depend on the data those studies generate. Individual small towns are not documented by governmental agencies or private organizations in such depth simply because there are not thousands of people who need the data. There aren't enough users to justify the costs of study.

For the person researching a small town, there are some good general resources and a few tactics that can be used to deal with this information inequity. Expect to make calls to find sources of data as well as the data themselves. In most cases the Resources Appendix will point you in the general direction of information you seek.

Your sources will reveal wonderful possibilities if you give them a chance. Remember Rule 2: *Allow enough time.*

Honor the Data That You Yourself Supply. Data, statistics, reports, and maps on parts of the country are only information. All the "correct" information in the world can't make you happy when you're not. If all the data you collect about a particular research topic say one thing but your heart says another, listen to your heart. It is trying to tell your head something for a reason. *Did you miss something?* Your heart must feel something that your stack of information doesn't yet reflect.

Use Rule 3: *Feelings are as important as facts.*

Break Down Big Questions into Small Ones. It's easy to get intimidated by the research you are facing. After all, these are big questions. What type of town do I want? What type of schools? How will I earn an income? What type of weather do I want? And above all, where do I find out these things? These are big questions about big topics, and the stakes are high. If you get the right answers, you'll find yourself living in a place that suits you beautifully. If not, it'll suit you less well than it could have. When a question starts to feel intimidating, break it into smaller, less intimidating pieces in a research "tree." (Picture a typical pine tree.) With your major topic at the top and the sources you'll contact at the bottom, it looks like this:

Major topic
<u>Subtopics</u>
Research questions
Information sources

As you answer the smaller, simpler questions at the bottom, you'll assemble answers to the major-topic question, piece-by-piece. For now, jot research trees you make on the back of your Employment and Quality-of-Life Worksheets. We'll cover how to keep track of the information you compile in a few pages. In your own research tree on employment, the subtopics, research questions, and information sources will probably differ from this sample's. Still, it will give you an understanding of how a research tree works:

What are my employment options in a small town?
    <u>What type of work could I do in a small town?</u>
        What type of jobs are available?
           Check with state or local employment agencies, look at want ads in
           local newspaper, contact a head hunter in the region.
        Are any of the possibilities what I want?
           Take an honest look at my desires. Talk with spouse.
        Will there be any growth or advancement possibilities?
           Check specific companies, local economic forecasts, ask around town.
    <u>How will moving to a small town affect my income?</u>
        How much will I be able to earn in a small town?
           Check with state and local employment agencies for job
           wage information, check with specific companies.
        Is that enough?
           Check our projected budget. Find out about benefits, state health plan
           possibilities, and insurance premiums. Discuss lifestyle changes with spouse.
    <u>What is the cost of employment in a small town?</u>
        Will I have to pay commuting expenses?
           Check map. What are the job opportunities in, or close to, a town we like?
        Will I have to pay for my own benefits?

*Check with specific employers. Find out what is standard practice
from unions, professional associations, state labor agencies.*

Will I need to buy nice clothes and pay for dry cleaning?

Chat with locals. Find out during job interviews.

Will I have some job flexibility?

Could I telecommute?

*Check maps. Discuss home-office idea with spouse. Get information
from alternative work and labor organizations. Talk with others who
are telecommuting.*

Could I job-share?

Explore this with specific companies.

How about flexible hours?

Ask the companies I interview with.

A lot of these sample research questions share the same research information source. That means that you will be able to use one source to answer multiple questions. You'll probably find this to be true about many of the research questions you ask.

Make a research tree for any question you feel needs it. Here are a few more sample research trees to jog your thinking.

What is the weather in the towns I'm considering?

What is the temperature there?

How hot and how cold does it get?

*National Oceanic and Atmospheric Administration (NOAA), state
department of agriculture.*

What are the average temperatures each month?

NOAA, state department of agriculture.

Are there frequent cold snaps or hot spells?

NOAA, state department of agriculture.

How much precipitation do each of these places get?

How much precipitation is there per year?

NOAA, state department of agriculture.

What is the average precipitation each month?

NOAA, state department of agriculture, local newspaper.

How much falls as rain and how much as snow?

NOAA, state department of agriculture.

What are the growing seasons there?

When is first and last frost?

Ask the locals, check with local newspaper.

What climate belt is the town in?

Check the gardeners' directories.

Is it really as dry as I've heard?

Ask the locals. Ask at the local nursery.

How about all the other climate factors?

What's the pollen count in the spring?

County department of agricultural, local health center, local medical groups/doctors.

Are there any local microclimates I should avoid?

Ask at the local nursery.

How does the public safety compare in places I'm considering?

What is the crime rate in these towns?

What is the rate of violent crime in this town?

State, local authorities. Also local newspaper.

Is the crime rate increasing? Steady? Decreasing?

State, local authorities. Newspaper.

Are the local authorities effective?

Read the newspaper. Ask the locals.

Are the schools safe?

Talk with teachers. Read the newspaper. Visit classrooms.

How good are the emergency services in these places?

How close is the nearest hospital?

Check the map. Drive the route and time it.

What is the ambulance response time?

State insurance commission. Local agencies.

What is the police response time?

Insurance commission. Local police department.

What is the fire department response time?

Insurance commission. Fire department.

What is the town environment like in general?

Are the streets well lit?

Drive around at night. Take a look.

Is the snow removal prompt?

Ask the locals.

Is the traffic flow well regulated?

Drive around enough to get a feel for traffic flow.

Are the parks safe?

Visit in the day, check lighting, maintenance.

How good are the schools in each of these places?

How do the scores, measures, and ratings of each town compare?

How is the school district rated?

State or local school authorities.

What is the graduation rate?

State or local school authorities.

What is the average class size?

State or local school authorities.

What are the test scores for the high school?

State or local school authorities.

How about the other indicators?

Is the discipline effective?

Visit the classrooms. Talk with teachers.

Is there a good sports program for girls?

Ask the principal. Talk with the physical education instructors.

Is there computer technology training?

Ask the principal.

Is the school system itself healthy?

What percentage of high school graduates go on to college?

State or local school authorities.

Is the school tax base strong and dependable?

Talk with local school board, read the newspaper, ask around.

What is the real estate market like in each of these towns?

What housing prices and values can we expect?

How do housing prices compare with rental prices?

Track in newspaper. Check with real estate agents.

Are there good homes available?

Get real estate listings and check out likely houses.

What are typical costs per square foot?

Calculate from the real estate listings.

What are the local expenses associated with housing?

What are the local tax rates?

Contact local tax assessor for rates.

What are the local utility rates?

Contact local utilities and get rate sheets.

Is it cheapest to heat with wood, electricity, or oil?

Ask real estate agents, and ask around.

<u>Are there other local issues that affect housing prices?</u>

Is there local zoning? Is it enforced effectively?

Ask at city hall, the county building. Read newspapers.

Are houses in town on sewers or septic systems?

Check with real estate agents.

Is there a tree ordinance in town?

Check with city planning.

For indicators of a town's financial stability, review the list of questions in Chapter 3, on the economic health of small cities. These apply as well to small towns and can be broken down into research trees.

Consolidate Your Worksheets

If you are the type of person who organizes the food in your cupboards alphabetically and sorts odds and ends into labeled containers, you might tend to over-organize your research. Keep in mind Rule 4:

Be open-minded and flexible.

Now that you have an idea of how to go about researching, the next step is to make sure you have a system for effectively using the information you receive. If you have all the elements organized and ready to go, you'll reach a conclusion faster. Imagine leaving for a trip without adequate preparation. You barely get out of the driveway and have to go back for your toothbrush. Then at the gas station you wonder whether you turned the iron off, and back you go again. Five miles down the road, it hits you that your checkbook is almost out of checks, and home you go once more. (Does this sound familiar?) You can avoid false starts and frustrating delays by making sure you have things well organized at the outset.

○ **Sort and Combine Your Worksheets by Topic**

If your search for a new town involves others, it is time to combine similar worksheets. If you and your loved ones filled out Employment Worksheets in Chapter 6, gather all of them together regardless of priority (for now). Do the same with all of the Quality-of-Life Worksheets that you and the others in your group have filled out. You should have one big stack of worksheets. Now you're ready to integrate the worksheets to form an effective filter. The idea here is to sort all of the worksheets by attractive characteristic, combining those that touch on a similar topic.

Go through your worksheets and look at the topic of each one. Is there some overlap? That's what you're looking for. Do you have two or three that deal with the topic of weather? If so, paper clip them together. Do you have some that deal with schools? Clip them together. Any other similar topic? Clip them.

By putting together all of the similar or identical characteristics, you will save yourself a great deal of research time. If you can agree on an integrated description that allows you to merge several worksheets into one, grab a fresh worksheet and do so. Each time you can merge a few worksheets, you simplify your research.

What happens if you have worksheets dealing with similar topics and you want to merge them, but they have different priority rankings? For example, one person rates nearby fishing a must-have and another rates it a good idea. We suggest you let the highest rating take precedence. This approach ensures that everybody's worksheets end up being accorded the same or better priority as they were originally assigned.

What if conflict arises? What if one person wants to live near skiing but another never wants to touch a snow shovel again in her life? (There *are* small towns that satisfy both requirements!) The short answer to this is: back off for now. If combining certain worksheets causes conflict within your group, then leave those specific worksheets alone until later; build consensus on what you can and leave the rest until enough factors are known to create a context for any compromise required.

Take time to focus on getting better acquainted with the thinking of the others in your group. Don't second guess their opinions or concerns. It may have been a while since you've discussed in depth the topics that come up. This is not the time to try to change each other's thinking. By being open to each other's ideas and by really listening to what others are saying, you show respect and a willingness to work together. You'll be repaid later!

To Build Consensus, Listen Effectively

O **Arrange Your Worksheets by Priority**

Whether you're working in a group or working alone, you'll want to organize all of your worksheets so you can refer to them easily throughout your research and search process. Reorganize your worksheets according to the highest priority assigned to each single worksheet or paper-clipped set of similar worksheets, but this time in five stacks:

Stack 1. Employment must-haves
Stack 2. Quality-of-life must-haves
Stack 3. Very-desirable characteristics
Stack 4. Good-idea characteristics
Stack 5. Might-be-nice characteristics

(*Note*: Stacks 3, 4, and 5 include both Employment and Quality-of-Life Worksheets, while stacks 1 and 2 keep them separate.)

Now your stacks are ready to put into a filing system.

○ **Set Up a Filing System**

Have you heard the expression, "Opinions are like noses—everybody's got one?" Well, filing systems are like opinions. The problem is that most of us have noses that work much better than our filing systems. We suggest that you set up one that will hold lots of data but be nearly effortless to use. There are a thousand different ways to go about this, but here are three basic systems that are simple and inexpensive, and that work well.

The File Folder System. Take each one of your Quality-of-Life and Employment Worksheets and staple it to the inside of its own file folder. When you receive a piece of information, all you have to do is drop it into the right file folder. This system is simple and cheap.

Three Simple Filing Systems

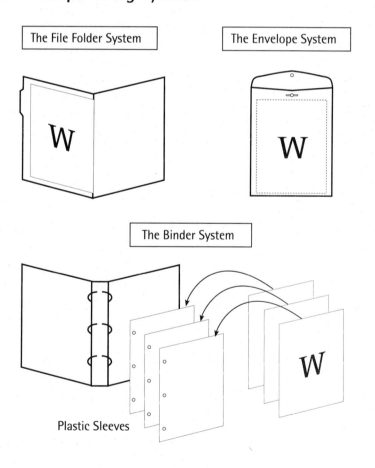

The File Folder System

The Envelope System

The Binder System

Plastic Sleeves

The Envelope System. Get some rubber cement and glue each of your Quality-of-Life and Employment Worksheets to its own big manila envelope. Each piece of information goes in the envelope with the appropriate worksheet on the outside.

The Binder System. This system is a little more expensive, but it has some advantages. Get a big three-ring binder, some binder dividers, and some of those clear plastic sleeves that are open at the top and are punched to go into a binder. Put each of your Quality-of-Life and Employment Worksheets in its own plastic sleeve. Any information or notes go in the plastic sleeve with the appropriate worksheet. This system is portable, and all your information can be kept together.

Whichever filing system you use, it's important to order your worksheets from most important (must-haves) to least important (might-be-nices).

○ **Create a Research Bulletin Board**

It's extremely useful to get a big map of the United States or the particular region you're considering and pin it up on a large bulletin board or wall that you can easily get to. Good map stores have many kinds of specialized maps as well, and you can mail-order topographical and aerial maps from the U.S.G.S. (see *Maps* in the Resource Appendix at the back of this book). Depending on your needs, you may also want to pin up smaller maps showing climatic, geological, or certain demographic data of interest to you.

To help create a visual portrait of what you're looking for, collect pictures of scenes you'd like to see in your new hometown and pin these up around your map. During your research you can add such data as lists of clubs related to your hobby and magnet schools of interest to your kids, by location. Mark towns that meet all must-haves with colored pins, if you like. Add clippings of real estate ads, meaningful headlines from small town newspapers, and personal notes and business cards from people you contact in small towns. These will be great motivators to get you through the research phase.

Organize the Information as It Comes In

It is just as important to have a methodical plan to make use of the information that comes in as it is to have a methodical plan to acquire it. When your research leads you to new information, ask:

A Research Bulletin Board

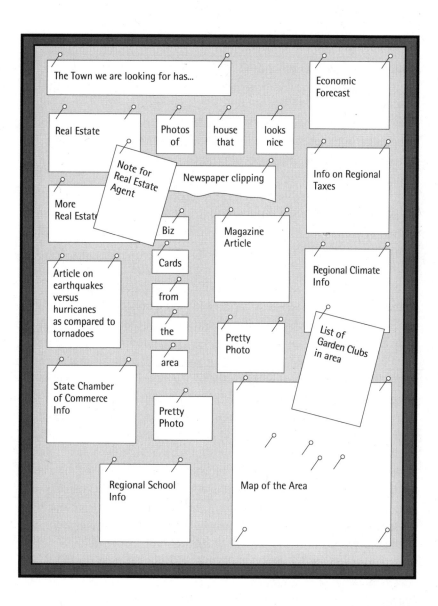

Dedicate an accessible bulletin board to your small-town search, and add new pictures and data as you go.

What is this information about? When you get a piece of information, take a look at all of it. Remember that one piece of information can help answer several questions; read through it thoroughly. Make sure you understand what attractive characteristics the information actually concerns.

Where should I file it? File your information so that there is a way to retrieve it by worksheet for each of the characteristics it might affect. You can do this by photocopying it and filing a copy with each of the Employment or Quality-of-Life Worksheets it relates to. Or you can file it with the worksheet that it mainly applies to and write a note on others that says something like, "See the letter from the State Department of Commerce that's in the envelope with the employment home office information." If one or two characteristics you're researching have many bits of related data recorded in other characteristics' files, a cross-reference list of those files with a few words describing the data for each may be enough of a prompt to your memory. Just don't depend on remembering with no prompts at all—you are going to collect a lot of data.

Cross-reference the information and material you receive, using any basic method. It's especially important to head off frustration from data loss this way if day-to-day organization isn't one of your natural strengths.

Tip

Often, it's hard to know right away just how valuable new information might be. As your information comes in, put what appears useful, together with your own notes about it, in your filing system, but don't throw the rest out yet. Put it in a box. You may find some of it valuable later in your search, particularly if any of your priorities or needs change.

The Search Begins

Take a minute to look through your filing system. You don't know the name or location of the small town yet, but what your files really contain is a template of its identity. You're ready to embark on the second half of your adventure. You have everything ready for the search for your ideal small town.

Here is an overview of the steps you'll take to search out ten or fewer candidate towns from entire regions. The search process takes place in three general stages, after you write in ranked must-haves and other attractive characteristics on Search Worksheets A and B.

In Step 10 you'll determine on your map the regions within which you are most likely to find your perfect town. Your must-haves alone will probably be limiting enough to determine the likely regions. This part of

The Search Worksheet Part A

Patience + persistence = good research.

Step 11 Name the likely towns.

Step 9 List the employment must-haves, the most geographically limiting first.

1 _____

2 _____

3 _____

4 _____

5 _____

Step 12 Investigate and evaluate each town.

Step 9 List quality-of-life must-haves, the most geographically limiting first.

1 _____

2 _____

3 _____

4 _____

5 _____

Step 10 On a map of the entire area you are considering, outline regions that do not meet your must-haves and mark them out of the running. Draw another color border around those that do. Apply as many must-haves and other characteristics as necessary to pinpoint a researchable number of likely towns.

The Search Worksheet Part B

Step 11 Name the likely towns.

Step 9 List the other attractive characteristics, in order of importance.

Step 12 Evaluate each town.

the process you can do entirely on the map, perhaps using worksheets to check the order of your must-haves. You'll indicate regions by both crossing off those that do not meet your must-haves and outlining those that do. You'll eventually want to mark, maybe with colored pushpins, the towns that you determine in this process also meet all of your must-haves.

In Step 11 you'll zero in on candidate towns within the pursuable regions. At this point you'll be marking +, √, or – in the squares for each town that you name on the worksheets. By eliminating any town that fails to meet a single one of your must-haves, you'll narrow the number of towns to about ten. These are the serious candidates, which you'll research more fully in Step 12.

You might want to vary this approach, depending on the complexity and constraints of your needs. If you are most constrained by your employment must-haves, you'll start with them. If you are retired or have less constraining employment requirements, you'll start with your quality-of-life must-haves. If after considering all of your geographically limiting must-haves you are still looking at dozens of possible small towns, you'll screen them with the most geographically limiting of your other attractive characteristics before you intentionally move on to Step 12.

You'll work generally from Worksheet A to Worksheet B and from top to bottom on each page. Your research will probably allow you to eliminate several regions and to fill in several squares at once, though; research tends not to be linear. Since it is not, and since you need to research first the characteristics that will eliminate the largest territory so as not to waste time, the worksheets are organized to help you keep the most restrictive elements uppermost. This is why you order the must-haves from most to least geographically restrictive and, for Step 12, order the other characteristics by their importance to you. Researching your most geographically restrictive must-haves first will save you from further researching places that you wouldn't possibly choose in the end.

○ **Step 9: Rank Your Must-Haves by the Geographic Limits They Impose**

In your research files, envelopes, or binder, review for any geographic limits dictated by each of the Employment and Quality-of-Life Worksheet characteristics you determined to be must-haves. Which must-haves can only be satisfied within one specific geographic area and not within any others? These are your most limiting, the characteristics to apply first. Those that can be satisfied in more than one area, or in one area that's very large, are less geographically limiting.

Here are some examples:

• *Our town must be less than two hours drive from Deb's mother's house* is more geographically limiting than *our town must have access to a major airport.* Why? Because Deb's mother only lives in one place, but there are major airports all over the country.

• *Our town must have a top-notch music conservatory* is probably more geographically limiting than *our town must have a good school system.* In most areas of the country there are probably far fewer top-notch music conservatories than good school systems.

Mapping the Geographical Limitations of Your Search

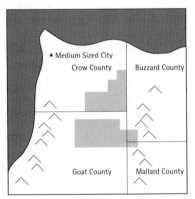

Snow-Free Area

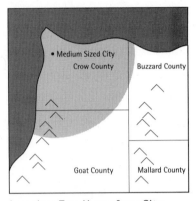

Less than Two Hours from City

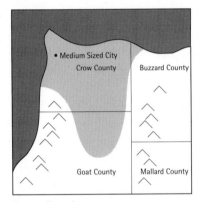

Good School Districts

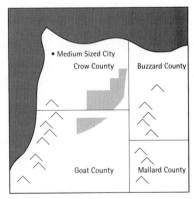

Areas of Overlap

Your own geographical limtations may be simpler than this example, or more complex. They may cover three states or a small valley. But if you use them to your advantage, they can make your search both faster and easier.

• *Our town must have a mild climate with no snow* is more geo-graphically limiting than *our town must be within two hours of a city, for Betty's business.* There are lots of small towns within two hours of a city, but far fewer of them also have mild, snowless climates.

• *Our town must be right on the seacoast* is more limiting than *our town must be smaller than 3,000 in population.* There are thousands of towns across the nation that are smaller than 3,000 in population, but comparatively few of them are right on the seacoast.

There may be some gray areas. If you can't say how limiting a must-have is, rank it below the ones that are clearly limiting. This will help you zero in. Soon you'll have research data to help you decide.

When you've ranked all the must-haves in your filing system, write them top to bottom on a copy of Search Worksheet A in the same order.

Describe Your Town in One Sentence

Look at your must-haves. Read them to yourself, in order, from most to least limiting. Now write a single sentence from the phrases that you can use to describe to yourself, or to anyone who may ask you during your research, exactly what you are looking for in a small town. Post it on your research bulletin board. This will come in handy. Being able to accurately describe what you seek is a major step on the way to finding it. Here's one example:

My kind of town is a small, lively college town in a mild climate with no snow, within a two-hour drive of a city, with a good nursing home and with good schools for the kids.

If your must-haves change during your search, simply write out a new sentence. Nothing's set in concrete yet.

Once your must-haves are written in on Search Worksheet A, take a moment and write all of the rest of your attractive characteristics on Search Worksheet B. Take up your very desirable, good-idea, and might-be-nice stacks in order, writing down each characteristic top to bottom in the left-hand column of the Search Worksheet from your top-priority to your lowest-priority characteristics. Simple preference rather than geographic or other limits apply here.

○ **Mind Merge**

As we suggested before when you sorted and combined your Employment and Quality-of-Life Worksheets, if your group has conflicts over these rankings, let the highest rating take precedence. For example, if one person rates a good bookstore as a very desirable characteristic yet another rates it as only might-be-nice, then list "good bookstore" among the very desirable elements on your Search Worksheet. If there are many

The Search Worksheet Part A

Patience + persistence = good research.

Step 11 Name the likely towns.

Melton | Slader | Ellis Ferry | Felk | Rock Ridge | Webster | Pine Creek

Step 9 List the employment must-haves, the most geographically limiting first.

1 *Adequate income to maintain our lifestyle.*

2 *A more interesting job for Fred.*

3

4

5

Step 12 Investigate and evaluate each town.

Step 9 List quality-of-life must-haves, the most geographically limiting first.

1 *A good climate with four real seasons.*

2 *A good school system.*

3 *A town with 5,000 to 10,000 people.*

4 *It has to be a safe place.*

5

Step 10 On a map of the entire area you are considering, outline regions that do not meet your must-haves and mark them out of the running. Draw another color border around those that do. Apply as many must-haves and other characteristics as necessary to pinpoint a researchable number of likely towns.

The Search Worksheet Part B

Step 11 Name the likely towns.

	Melton	Slader	Ellis Ferry	Felk	Rock Ridge	Webster	Pine Creek

Step 9 List the other attractive characteristics, in order of importance.

Step 12 Evaluate each town.

	Melton	Slader	Ellis Ferry	Felk	Rock Ridge	Webster	Pine Creek
Clean air.							
A lower cost of living.							
More time for the kids and fun stuff.							
A telecommuting job for Deb.							
A job that Fred likes.							
A town where we can walk to work.							
A nice old Victorian house to live in.							
A friendly neighborhood.							
Deb can work part time.							
A town with a slow growth rate.							
Within 500 miles of friends and family.							
Place where Fred could run a photography business on the side.							
A lot of big old trees on the streets.							
A house with a private yard.							
Room for horses.							

The Search Worksheet Part B

Step 11 Name the likely towns.

Melton | Slader | Ellis Ferry | Felk | Rock Ridge | Webster | Pine Creek

Step 9 List the other attractive characteristics, in order of importance.

Step 12 Evaluate each town.

	Melton	Slader	Ellis Ferry	Felk	Rock Ridge	Webster	Pine Creek
A good piano teacher for Stu.							
A place that's closer to skiing / camping.							
A good Chinese restaurant.							
Close to good fishing.							
A town with good live music.							

rankings that conflict, however, you might want to take another approach and aim for equal representation. Assign a limit to the number of items each one is allowed to list at each priority level. For example, allow five very desirable characteristics per person. This will help your group avoid the "you're getting more than me" trap.

To recap, the goal of Steps 9, 10, and 11 is to generate a list of towns that is short enough to research thoroughly and that meets every one of your must-have conditions. The goal of step 12 is to learn enough about each of those towns that you can fill in *most* of the squares under each town with a +, √, or – evaluation. The towns that have most of the characteristics you want compose your shortlist.

○ **Step 10: Make the Calls, Write the Letters, Get the Search Process Rolling**

The way to narrow the search geography is to begin the research. Start with the most geographically limiting must-have at Step 9 on your Search Worksheet A. Contact or look up each Step 8 resource on the Employment or Quality-of-Life Worksheet for this must-have. Find out what you need to know. Keep a record of phone calls and copies of any letters you write so that you know when to follow up with nonresponders.

Write down at Step 8 any additional resources as you discover them.

At this early stage of your search, you're likely to receive a lot of general information, such as national rainfall figures or national school test scores. Sort the information that is not specific to geography by its topic, and file it to use later in filling in the worksheet squares for towns. Sort the information that does refer to a certain area or town by its location, and use it to draw in borders on your map. Meanwhile, start the ball rolling on the second must-have, then the third, and so on down through all your employment and quality-of-life must-haves.

As you work your way down your list of must-haves, certain towns may emerge quickly as strong candidates. In Step 11 you'll list them across the top of the Search Worksheet, but concentrate at this point on simply narrowing the number of regions rather than seeking specific towns.

When a Town Fails One of Your Must-Have Tests	Stop researching it. Drop it like a hot poker. Don't expend one more second of your time on it. You'll never live there, so put your time and energy into further researching the towns that do satisfy all your must-have requirements. You'll end up living in one of those!

Continue to clarify the geographic boundaries within which you know a must-have can be satisfied. Take a highlighter or a pen and mark those boundaries on the map on your research bulletin board. Add boundaries to your map as each successive must-have further limits your search area.

When you're done researching all of your must-haves, your bounded area may be a set of perfect, concentric circles like a bull's eye, or irregular, overlapping blob shapes. It may be the size of a large state, several counties, or one school district or rural zone. The smaller the area bounded—your "inner circle"—the easier your search will be from this point forward.

O **Use Your Other Attractive Characteristics to Narrow the Search**

What if the inner circles that your must-haves have generated on your map hold fifty (or more!) small towns, each of which satisfies all of your geographically limiting must-have conditions? Clearly, it would take months to do in-depth research on fifty or a hundred individual small towns. After all, the idea is to find and choose a small town sometime before your life insurance pays off.

At the top of your Step 10 list should be a few characteristics that almost became must-haves in an earlier chapter. Think about which of these high-priority characteristics are most geographically limiting and could be used to weed out the most towns at once. Research them and use the results to narrow the field. Continue to gather data until you zero in on ten or so candidate towns; fewer is better, since this too eases the remaining research.

Some people prefer to fill in evaluation squares the minute they receive new information. Some prefer to read it, digest it, and file it, recording it at a regular weekly or other time. Neither approach is a problem. Just make sure you don't jump the gun and make an evaluation based on incomplete information, or lose track of information you have to record. If you receive additional information when you've already filled the applicable square, take a moment to reevaluate.

Rule 7:
Rules are made to be broken.

Here are examples of geographically limiting attractive characteristics that have research resources you can use to screen a number of towns at once.

An attractive, older town that has character.
Use this to narrow your search by ruling out any small towns that were incorporated after the year 1940, with a series of short, direct calls to state departments of land use and development or to county planning commissions. This will automatically knock out any towns on your map that are those small, soulless "strip style" towns from the 1950s or 1960s.

The Search Worksheet Part A

Must-Haves

Patience + persistence = good research.

Step 11 Name the likely towns.

Towns: Melton, Slader, Ellis Ferry, Felk, Rock Ridge, Webster, Pine Creek

Step 9 List the employment must-haves, the most geographically limiting first.

Step 12 Investigate and evaluate each town.

	Melton	Slader	Ellis Ferry	Felk	Rock Ridge	Webster	Pine Creek
1 Adequate income to maintain our lifestyle.	✓	−	+	✓	✓	+	✓
2 A more interesting job for Fred.	✓	✓	+	✓	✓	+	✓
3							
4							
5							

Step 9 List quality-of-life must-haves, the most geographically limiting first.

	Melton	Slader	Ellis Ferry	Felk	Rock Ridge	Webster	Pine Creek
1 A good climate with four real seasons.	✓	✓	+	✓	+	+	✓
2 A good school system.	✓	−	+	✓	+	✓	✓
3 A town with 5,000 to 10,000 people.	✓	✓	✓	✓	✓	✓	✓
4 It has to be a safe place.	✓	✓	−	+	+	✓	−
5							

Step 10 On a map of the entire area you are considering, outline regions that do not meet your must-haves and mark them out of the running. Draw another color border around those that do. Apply as many must-haves and other characteristics as necessary to pinpoint a researchable number of likely towns.

The Search Worksheet Part B

Other Attractive Characteristics

Step 11 Name the likely towns.

Step 9 List the other attractive characteristics, in order of importance.

Step 12 Evaluate each town.

Characteristic	Melton	Slader	Ellis Ferry	Felk	Rock Ridge	Webster	Pine Creek
Clean air.	+	+		✓	+	✓	✓
A lower cost of living.	✓	✓		−	✓	✓	✓
More time for the kids and fun stuff.	✓			−	✓	+	
A telecommuting job for Deb.		−		✓	+		
A job that Fred likes.	✓			✓	+		
A town where we can walk to work.	+			−	+	✓	
A nice old Victorian house to live in.				✓	✓	+	
A friendly neighborhood.	+			✓	+	✓	
Deb can work part time.				✓	✓		
A town with a slow growth rate.	+			−	+	✓	
Within 500 miles of friends and family.	✓			✓	✓	−	
Place where Fred could run a photography business on the side.					−	✓	
A lot of big old trees on the streets.	+			+	✓	+	
A house with a private yard.							
Room for horses.	✓				+	✓	

The Search Worksheet Part B

Other Attractive Characteristics

Step 11 Name the likely towns.

Melton | Slader | Ellis Ferry | Felk | Rock Ridge | Webster | Pine Creek

Step 9 List the other attractive characteristics, in order of importance.

Step 12 Evaluate each town.

Characteristic	Melton	Slader	Ellis Ferry	Felk	Rock Ridge	Webster	Pine Creek
A good piano teacher for Stu.				✓	✓		
A place that's closer to skiing / camping.	✓			+	+	+	
A good Chinese restaurant.	+			✓	−	✓	
Close to good fishing.	✓			✓	✓	✓	
A town with good live music.				+	−	−	

A town with ethnic diversity.
Check the *1990 Census Report* and other resources to rule out any towns that have minimal or no ethnic diversity.

A town with good electronic telecommuting potential.
Check with local phone companies to find which towns have digital switching equipment and fiber optic lines or satellite communications.

○ **Step 11: Write in Ten (or So) Likely Candidate Towns**

To distill the choices to no more than ten or so specific small towns, continue to narrow the number of towns by applying your must-haves, your geographic-limitations map, and your prioritized list of other attractive characteristics. It may take awhile to zero in on the candidate towns you're going to research thoroughly. That's OK. You want enough choices to feel that your options are not too limited, but not so many as to be overwhelming.

Remember to work from top to bottom on the forms. Move on to screening a town by your other attractive characteristics only after it has met every single one of your must-haves.

○ **Step 12: Investigate Your Candidate Towns**

Continue your research. Find out everything you can about each of your candidate towns. Make lots of calls, write lots of letters, and fill up your research bulletin board and your filing system. Contact the resources you listed in Step 8, add to them as you go, and gather as much information as you can. You might already have piled up several file folders or maybe even several boxes of information as background for all the symbols filling in the squares.

Obviously, it's very important to successfully complete all the research on your must-haves. But as mentioned, you may not be able to fill in every little detail on the less important characteristics. In truth, you don't need to. You can find an excellent town even if there are a few holes in your research. The trick is to keep the holes small and to be aware that they exist.

How do you know, then, when your hard-data research is done? When you have enough squares filled to be able to evaluate and compare your candidate towns. You'll have enough conclusions from hard-data comparisons that you can turn over the remaining decisions to your feelings. Because this is easier to recommend than to do, we help you shift to making decisions with soft data in the next chapter.

CHAPTER 9

The Shortlist Worksheet:
Focusing on the Finalists

Congratulations. You're over the hump. You have just spent weeks or perhaps months trying to remember which piece of information went with which small town. You and your loved ones have probably had some of your most soul-searching discussions ever. We certainly did. We also found that we could spend hours on the phone chasing one small, simple scrap of information—then the next day be dazed when a one-minute phone call resulted in a UPS delivery of ten pounds of computer print-out. Like us, you have probably taken a close look at your livelihood and asked yourself some fundamental questions about its place in your life. And if you're anything like us, you had a couple of real bases loaded, bottom-of-the-ninth arguments. So smile. The worst is behind you now.

The goal of this chapter is to narrow still further the list of candidate small towns you discovered through your research in the last chapter. You'll use a Shortlist Worksheet to compile each town's benefits and drawbacks. You'll also write down the questions you still have about each of your finalists. In the next chapter we'll help you organize a visit to several towns. And after the visit? The search is over. Only the final choice remains. But before you start on the Shortlist Worksheets (which won't require anything like the amount of work the last worksheets did), we need to talk about the inside of your brain a little.

You Have Two Brains

Your brain has two lobes, the right lobe and the left. They both look pretty much alike, but they serve you somewhat differently. Here's the basic difference: You do your income tax with your left brain. But your taste in neckties or handbags comes from your right. The left brain is supposed to handle unemotional, analytical, objective matters. The right brain is supposed to handle whatever's emotional, subjective, or artistic. Though no decisions are ever made wholly from the left or the right, many are made with respect only for logic.

In truth, you could probably move to just about any of your candidate towns right this moment and be at least reasonably happy, since they had to pass some rigorous logical tests even to stay on your Search Worksheet. But the point of all this work isn't just to find a small town in which you can be reasonably happy. Not at all. The point of the whole book is to help you find the one small town that is *extraordinarily* well suited to your wants and needs. The next step toward that goal is to fill in the inevitable gaps that logic is unable to fill.

The left brain says:

How much of a raise do I think I can get?

The right brain says:

Is this the time to ask, or is the old buzzard still in a bad mood?

The left brain says:

Moving to a small town will mean 16.3 percent less income.

But the right brain says:

Moving to a small town may mean we keep our sanity.

The left brain says:

It's impractical, even if it is beautiful.

But the right brain says:

It's beautiful. Who cares if it's impractical.

The left brain says:

Chocolate is a dangerous chemical compound that should carry a warning label.

But the right brain says:

There is no life without chocolate.

The left brain says:

I should go to the opera because I always see my major clients there.

But the right brain says:

I wonder if they all hate opera as much as I do?

The Difference Between Your Left Brain and Right Brain

Until now you have been doing predominantly left-brain work: organizing, prioritizing, researching, and analyzing. You've been weighing facts against each other and then seeking yet other facts based on those evaluations. This has all been necessary; difficult at times, but necessary. You wouldn't have been able to get this far without putting a lot of miles on your left brain.

In this chapter, it's time to shift lobes. Let your left brain start to cool off and get your right brain warmed up. This notion of allowing your feelings a role in such a big decision is a little scary. After all, most people are raised to think that the best decisions are based in cool, unemotional, purely rational thinking.

We are no exception to this. It took awhile to get comfortable with the idea that if we relied on the hard data without our feelings and intuition, we risked relocating to a town that met our statistical objectives but didn't have the right chemistry. We reminded ourselves continually that the towns we were considering had already passed our rigorous hard-data tests. They were already just fine as far as our left brains were concerned, or they wouldn't be still under consideration. We could comfortably switch to right-brain mode and explore less tangible elements, those that would ensure emotionally as well as logically that the town would fit us.

Now it's time to whittle your list down to the three to five towns that are your clear front-runners. You'll do this with right brain/left brain weeding, solidified by mind merges and reality checks.

....

Rule 3 is applicable here: *Feelings are as important as facts.*

○ **Compare Your Likely Candidates**

Look at your Search Worksheets from the last chapter. There, stretched across the top, are the ten towns, more or less, on which you've done considerable research. By now you probably have a feeling for which towns are the front-runners and which ones are toward the back of the pack. As you compare their marks, are there a few towns that look better or worse than you expected? Look at all of the columns, allowing yourself time to let the information sink in. It's a lot of data to compare. Of course, the more pluses there are under any town's name, the more closely that town matches your needs. Note as well that the more of these pluses are high up in the column, the better that town matches your really important needs. Be wary of any town that has a lot of minuses high in the column, and don't worry as much about minuses way at the bottom.

....

Even at this stage of this search process, you may come across other towns that you just want to investigate. If so, go ahead. Remember Rule 7: *Rules are made to be broken.*

○ **Pick Your Finalist Towns**

This is the point in the process when you narrow your search to a few exceptional candidates, the ones worth serious visits. If you're moving with a group, work individually for awhile, then work together.

Are there two or three towns that really make you want to start packing boxes and sending out change of address notes? Specifically, which towns have the most pluses adjacent to the must-haves? Which ones seemed the most interesting as you were researching? Which ones have the most pluses high in the attractive-characteristics column? The fewest negative marks? The best look on paper, the best *feel*? The right questions to ask are any that evoke a sure response. You want to both use your head and trust your gut reactions. Circle the names of the few towns at the top of your Search Worksheet that you like most at this point.

○ **Mind Merge**

If you are making a small-town move with others—a spouse, children, a business associate—you'll want to do a mind merge here. This is an obvious time to synchronize. Sit down individually with the Search Worksheets and make your own right brain/left brain choices. Each of you, refrain from influencing the others. Put on a poker face until everyone's done. We'll make a prediction here: If you've been doing a lot of formal or informal mind merges all along, you'll be surprised by how many of your choices are identical.

Creating your shortlist is a major step. All the towns that you do not select at this point are permanently out of the running. We make two suggestions:

Even after choosing towns for your shortlist, reconsider your choices. Give yourself a few days to change your mind. Use your right brain to look over the towns you've circled on your Search Worksheet. Do they feel like the right ones? Are there any towns on your Shortlist Worksheets that don't feel like they belong? Are there any that are missing? If so, make the necessary adjustments. Okay, now switch over to your left brain (that's the income tax side) and revert to your usual cool, unemotional, analytical self. Look hard at your Search Worksheets. Ponder. Analyze. Calculate. Do the towns that you picked pass this inspection too? If not, make the changes you need to.

Have confidence in the choices you make. You have been considering these choices for quite a while. You are probably quite comfortable with most of the towns that you are ready to declare your shortlist finalists. Especially after the right brain/left brain review, know that you've done your best to make the right selection.

Still Too Many Towns?

If you are still looking at more than three towns—maximum five or six if you really want that many to visit—you will probably want to do more thinning. The goal, ideally, is to end up feeling that you have a few really excellent choices.

If you are moving with others, there is a pretty good chance that you're not yet down to this "few." Let's say for example that there are three of you. Together, you have eight contenders that you want to whittle down to five shortlist slots. That means you want to lose three towns. You've all tried civilized discussion and it just isn't working. What do you do?

Get everybody together at a table next to your research bulletin board with all the interesting small-town stuff on it. Have your research files handy. Bring an open mind. Try this consensus-building exercise:

Each of you picks three towns you're ready to eliminate, for three lists of three. If there are two or three that all of you agree should go, of course, problem solved. But if you come up short of complete consensus, there still has to be at least one town that two of you agree on. Eliminate that one, and repeat the process as many times as necessary to reduce the number of towns to three or so. Have faith. You'll get there.

○ Reality Check

Several chapters ago we advised you to put aside conflicts of values, pending research results. Now that the hard data are in and you're ready to declare a shortlist, have everyone's needs been met? Is there one of you who feels left out because his or her most favorite small town was unceremoniously dumped from the shortlist? If so, you may need to take some extra time now to resolve conflicts. A little grease now will save a lot of squeaking and overheating later.

When you have about five finalist towns, put the name of each at the top of a Shortlist Worksheet. If two or three were chosen more with your right brain and two or three more with your left, that's good. It gives you variety in the towns you'll choose from.

Right-Brain Research

Now it's time to become intimately familiar with each of the short-list favorites. The research you need to do next is right-brain research. It's fun. It's easy. And you don't have to get out a calculator.

The Shortlist Worksheet

Before you start this Worksheet, repeat Rule 3 out loud:

Feelings are as important as facts.

Step 13 List the benefits of this town:

_____

_____

_____

_____

_____

_____

_____

Step 14 List the drawbacks of this town:

_____

_____

_____

_____

_____

Step 15 List any remaining questions about this town:

_____

_____

_____

_____

_____

_____

The goal of this right-brain research is to get a feel for each of the small towns on your shortlist, to answer all of the soft questions that will help you determine your comfort with the towns' personalities. Which one has the group of people with which you'll be most compatible? Which ones are true communities, not just a bunch of people living near each other? In short, the goal of this right-brain research is to answer the question, which place feels like home?

What makes right-brain research enjoyable when left-brain research can be about as much fun as having your teeth cleaned? You do left-brain research to get the objectively correct answer, right-brain research to get the subjectively correct one. Another way to think of it is in terms of cooking: Finding and measuring ingredients for a recipe is like left-brain research. It's a necessary nuisance. But tasting the sauce to figure out which spices to add is a form of right-brain research. It's creative and it's subjective. Besides, everybody likes tasting something really good right off the top of the stove.

Here are the tools we suggest you start with. Clear your research bulletin board and pin the names of your final shortlist towns across the top. Organize under these names any materials you already have on the towns. As you contact the resources listed below, add the most useful and intriguing pieces of information you receive. Besides pictures and articles you clip, pin up favorite quotes from local folks, real estate brochures, church newsletters, and anything that gives you a feeling for the town. Good or bad, it's all fair game. After a few weeks you'll have a fair image of each town.

Local Maps. Maps are wonderful. Post them where everybody can look at them. They can give you a strong sense of a place even if you have not yet been able to set foot there. Most of us are better map readers than we give ourselves credit for being.

Maps come in a huge variety. Virtually everyone is familiar with road maps. They can tell you where the minor roads are, where the major roads are, or where the freeway access is. It's not a bad idea to get a street map for every small community you're considering. That way you can find the location of, for example, a proposed building or contested subdivision that you read about in the local newspaper.

Street maps are just a start—many other maps and charts are available too. The entire nation is covered by U.S. Geological Survey topographic maps. These maps provide vast amounts of information about elevation, topography, watercourses, vegetation, and geology. Ten minutes spent inspecting such a map can yield great understanding of the natural attributes of an area. Are you considering a community near an airport? The Federal Aviation Agency has detailed aerial charts of the entire country. They show every airport, and they give a good picture of the local terrain. If you are considering a town near a major body of water, you might want to get the National Oceanographic and Atmospheric Administration (NOAA) chart of the area. We even found a poster with a satellite image of the area we eventually moved to. Even though it is taken from space, it shows the areas of different vegetation, the paths of high-tension lines through the forest, and even the roof of a very large warehouse.

Local Newspapers. Find out which local newspapers serve your small towns. Write for recent sample issues, or subscribe to each of them for a month or two. It'll take you that long to start to get the flavor of each place. Small-town newspapers are invaluable. Each line will give you the day-to-day news of the community: local political issues, what houses rent for, whether the city council or the county government functions well and fairly or is dominated by one interest group or another.

Read between the lines and you'll get the scent of the community. Check whether the letters to the editor are reasoned and tolerant or whether the town is divided into feuding Hatfield and McCoy factions. Lots of activities probably indicate community spirit. The social and political tone of the editorials may match your own or conflict sharply with your beliefs, which is of interest in itself but may also suggest the degree of diversity commonly tolerated.

Keep a set of scissors handy. When you see an article, an ad, or even a government notice that is of interest, cut it out and file it, or post it on your research bulletin board.

Community Newsletters. Literally dozens of small-town organizations produce newsletters: churches, community recreation programs, sports clubs, community service organizations, music clubs, local chamber orchestras, model railroad societies, model airplane clubs, square dance societies, artists' guilds, cooking clubs, antique car clubs, experimental aircraft builders, and volunteer firefighters, to name a few.

Newsletters not only convey the flavor of an area, they tell you if it is quiet or lively. They are also a source of phone numbers, often with the names of the people you can call. They may not have specific information you seek, but there is every reason to bet that they will know where to direct you.

Local Political Information. No matter what area of the country you're considering, the Democrats and the Republicans will have arrived there before you. And there may be a host of other political organizations as well. Whatever your own beliefs, it is a good idea to get some indications of the local politics of groups across the spectrum. A little exploration here will tell you what the local issues happen to be, where the power is centered, and in which directions these might be shifting. It will tell you whether the tone of the politics is calm and reasoned or loud and aggressive.

Political Information Exercise	When you contact the political organizations in the area or areas you are considering, ask if they can send some samples of literature from the last campaign. That will suggest whether it was a clean campaign and who dealt best with which issues.

Most political pamphlets, too, have names and phone numbers. That's yet more people you can call to chat with, and maybe slip in a few tangential questions for which you haven't found information sources elsewhere.

Local Phone Books. Get the phone book for each of the small towns you are considering. Typically the local phone company will mail you one for a small fee. Phone books are windows into virtually every aspect of a small town's daily life. Call organizations, associations, and groups that are of interest to you; trying a few ways of networking by phone will suggest others.

Phone Book Exercise #1: Errands	Write down all the errands you had to run during the last few days. Now pick up the phone books and find out where in each of your shortlist towns you'd go to run the same errands. Can each town provide the minimum essentials itself? If not, how far will you have to travel to meet those needs?

Phone Book Exercise #2: Personal Interests	Let's say that your passion in life is gardening. Whatever your passion, it ranks right up there with food and shelter as a basic requirement for human existence. If it's gardening, look through the Yellow Pages for the range of local nurseries, and call one or two in each of your shortlist small towns. Tell them that you are thinking of moving to their town and ask them about the local climate, about roses, or whatever the area of their expertise that interests you. Are they friendly, knowledgeable, and forthcoming? Remember, you'll be spending a lot of time (and perhaps a lot of money) with the local purveyors if you move there. Which one made you feel most welcome? Do the same exploration for other personal interests.

As you seek out soft information, compare and contrast. Do any towns emerge as particularly strong? Use the Shortlist Worksheets to record your impressions.

○ **Step 13: List the Benefits of Each Town**

Gather your Shortlist Worksheets. Make sure there is one sheet for every town that made it onto your shortlist. By now, as you read newspapers and poke through the phone books from each of your short-list towns, you're developing a sense of the towns' personalities. You're beginning to have strong feelings about the benefits and drawbacks of each. You can record these in just a few words.

Any town that has made it this far in your search process must have a lot going for it. Write down everything that you already know excites you about the place. Every time your research reveals or verifies an important benefit about one of your shortlist towns, write it down. Here is an example:

List the benefits of this town:	Step 13
The weather looks really good.	We can walk to work.
There's a great job for Fred.	The neighbors sound friendly.
The schools seem quite good.	The growth rate is slow.
It is a safe town.	Lots of houses with barns for sale.
The air is very clean.	Close to mountains.
A good (telecommuting!) job for Deb.	

By the completion of this step you'll have some benefits that appear on every single worksheet and some entries that are unique to their particular small towns. These unique ones may very well be the tie-breakers.

○ **Step 14: List the Drawbacks of Each Town**

Write down the things that concern you or make you a little uncomfortable about each town, as you continue your research. Don't worry about why. Trust your intuition and write it down.

Your drawbacks list will probably be a shorter list than your benefits list, but it's important to record these too. As with the benefits, if you're deciding among three or four very closely matched small towns, it may be one of the relatively minor drawbacks that finally tips the scales.

Step 14 List the drawbacks of this town:

It looks pretty weak for work opportunities.

It doesn't seem to have anything exceptional going for it.

The people we spoke with weren't all that friendly.

It seems more developed than we thought.

○ **Step 15: List the Questions That Remain about Each Town**

Congratulations! This is the last step on the last worksheet. No painstaking research, no calculator work, and no scratch paper are required.

List the questions that you still have about each of your shortlist towns after your research–the ones that you can answer well only by standing on Main Street. You generate these just as Step 13 and Step 14. As you do your research, poke through phone books, and read the local newspapers from each of your shortlist towns, questions are bound to come to mind. When they do, write them down.

Step 15 List any remaining questions about this town:

Are there any properties with enough room for a horse?

If so, could we afford them?

How active is the community during the nontourist season?

Is that new shopping center outside town going to kill the old downtown stores?

Is it too windy?

Is Jenny going to be comfortable at the middle school?

○ **Reality Check: The Most Important One in the Book**

OK. Time out.

Take a hard, critical look at where you are. You have a shortlist of towns, each of which should be close to perfect for you. One of these almost-perfect towns can be expected to make you a happy home—if the elements of happiness you've researched are the ones that now count most for you. Ask yourself this question:

Does moving to a small town still feel like the right thing to do?

If it does, you can skip the rest of this reality check.

But what if you aren't really happy enough with any of your short-list small towns to imagine living in one of them? What if you or your loved ones are no closer to consensus than you were at the outset? What if your desires or your needs are substantially unmet by any of your short-list towns, or not one of them feels right?

If this is the case, you need to put on the brakes right now. You may be driving down the wrong road.

Ask yourself these questions. Answer honestly. The stakes are high.	**Reality-Check Exercise**
• Are you attempting to solve personal problems with a moving van?	
• Now that you have examined small-town life, do you find that you really are a city person at heart?	
• Have your needs changed since you started your small-town search?	
• Does small-town life present obstacles that are insurmountable, given your individual situation?	
• Is it genuinely not possible to reach a workable consensus on a move with your loved ones?	
• Will the living you are able to earn in a small town be adequate?	
• Is a small town the right dream but this the wrong time to pursue it?	
• Are you just too set in your ways to make the adjustment to a small community?	

If there's a red flag in your mind about moving, focus on it now. You really need to stop and think this whole small-town thing through. If you press ahead at this point you may find yourself with a different address and the same set of dissatisfactions. We wouldn't wish that on anybody. Consider these steps:

Backtrack. Check your path from the beginning of your search. Is there any point at which you missed some critical information? Did you fail to build adequate consensus at some critical point? Was there a point at which you were asking the wrong questions?

Do a mind merge. Gather your loved ones together. Be honest with each other. Are there members of your group who are resistant because they feel their needs will not be met in any of the shortlist small towns? If so, is there a point in the process to which you could return and incorporate their needs more completely? Will they always have the same objections to any small town, or are there experiences they believe not possible in such places that actually could be arranged?

Reconsider. Have you been planning an extreme change when all you need is a minor one? Perhaps you've been looking at small towns when small cities are better suited to your needs, or vice versa. Or if this is the wrong time for a move that you would still like to make, does any of your research suggest a better time?

No More Worksheets

Your formal research is done, both right brain and left brain. You've made a list that could be entitled *My Best Places to Live,* which exists in no other place, no book, no magazine. It's time to move into the decision phase. In the next chapter, we are going to do everything we can to encourage you to pay a visit to each town on your shortlist, and make your final decision with your heart.

CHAPTER 10

Which Town Feels Right?
Paying a Visit

Some things in life require your personal presence. Did you ever hear of newlyweds taking separate honeymoons? There are some things you just have to be there for, and one of them is visiting the town you intend to make your new home.

Until now we have encouraged you to be flexible in the search for your kind of town. We've even encouraged you to detour around the suggested process if it didn't fit your personal situation. By now you've probably used Rule 7, *Rules are made to be broken,* a few times. That's good. But this chapter is different. One thing that you have to do, with no exceptions, is:

> **You have to spend some time on Main Street before**
> **you decide that any town is right for you.**

Yes, it is possible that you could get lucky and choose the right small community sight unseen. But if you did so, it would be no more than blind luck. Do you really want to trust so important a choice to luck? Consider the odds of success, especially when as most big American cities have become more similar over the past decades, the personalities of American small towns have become more varied and individual.

The few people we have met who have *not* been happy with their new small town either moved sight unseen or made only a cursory visit. In fact, moving to a town without paying a visit is probably just about *the only* thing you could do this late in your search that might land you in the wrong town.

We can't state it too strongly: *Do not* make your final choice without first paying a visit. Even if it has to be a short one. Even if you can't take the whole family. Even if you have to skimp and save in order to afford it, a visit to the towns you are considering will save you from making less than the best decision.

The Purpose of Your Visits

Let's take stock of where you are by now. You're close, so close you might even be looking forward to packing boxes and moving. And by now you are probably itching to pick a town. In the preceding chapter you narrowed your choices to a shortlist of five or so favorites and listed for each its benefits, its drawbacks, and your remaining questions. The purpose of this chapter and your visits to your finalist towns is to confirm the benefits and drawbacks, to answer the questions, and in the process for something else to happen. The most important goal of your visit is to develop a feeling for each town.

Assessing the Feeling of Community in Your Shortlist Towns	How do the towns you're considering and the neighborhoods within them rate in terms of community? • Does the design of the houses, apartment buildings, and block encourage interaction? • How pedestrian-friendly are the streets? Are there enough sidewalks? • Can you travel where you need to go—work, school, shopping, etc.—on foot or by public transportation easily? • How strong is the neighborhood identity? Does the neighborhood publish its own newspaper? Support a community center? • Is there an active neighborhood association? Do its issues extend beyond keeping property values high? Does it reach out to other neighborhoods? • How active are local merchants in community affairs? • Are most businesses locally owned, so that owner-residents have a stake in the neighborhood? Do the people who work in the businesses live in the neighborhood? • Are there plenty of trees? What about community gardens? • Do you see a diversity of people—different ages, races, economic classes—and do these groups interact with each other? • Is there plenty of street life, and is it safe? • How, if at all, does the neighborhood welcome new residents and new businesses? From *Creating Community Anywhere,* by Carolyn Shaffer and Kristin Anundsen

Planning Your Visits

Obviously, if you now live only a few hours from each of the towns you're considering, it will be relatively easy to visit them all. But what if you're considering a town in Georgia, one in Maine, one in New Mexico, and one on the Idaho-Washington border? And you live in Chicago? And you have three children? And you don't have a whole lot of money?

Clearly, putting the entire family on a plane and making a circuit from Georgia to Maine to New Mexico to Idaho and back to Chicago is not a likely option. What should you do? The following questions and answers suggest a range of options.

Q: What if I can't afford to visit each of my shortlist towns?
A: Ideally, we encourage you to visit them all. Realistically, if you are like the Chicago resident described above, visiting every town on your shortlist could consume all of the funds you have earmarked to pay for your actual move. You could, for example, visit the two most promising ones, which would establish a basis of comparison. If visiting two is not possible, then visit the one that seems most promising.

Camping can sometimes reveal more about an environment than a motel stay, besides saving money. RV parks often have quite civilized showers, restrooms, and even laundry facilities, and may have spots for car campers.

Q: What if it turns out that the one town I can afford to visit isn't it?
A: Then save your money until you can afford to visit the next best town on your shortlist. Be patient. It's worth it.

Q: Who should I bring with me to visit the shortlist towns?
A: Ideally, everybody who will be making the move to your new home town should go. The more of you who have walked up and down each town's main streets, the better. Each of you will bring different observations and reactions to the final choice. If this is not possible you may have to delegate responsibility to one or two of the people in your group.

Consider including at least one older child in each visit to a shortlist town, even if you can't send the whole family. The adult who goes can be deputized to answer another adult's set of questions and concerns. The older child can be given the task of looking into the concerns of the other children and for reporting back to them. Why do it this way? A child may vehemently resist a parental edict to get ready to pack up and move. That same child may prove to be quite willing to accept the word of an older brother or sister that a particular town is totally cool.

If you are moving alone, you might consider bringing a friend or relative. It might be handy to have somebody off of whom you can bounce your opinions and observations. This person might be the one to pinch you and tell you that you're dreaming. Or maybe they'll pinch you and tell you that you're not dreaming.

Q: How long do I need to spend in each town?

A: The short answer is, *long enough to get a feel for the place.* And in practice, this can take less time than you might expect. If you do some pre-planning for your visit, and you are efficient with your time, three days may be enough. For most people, though, four days is the minimum to plan. If you have the time, shoot for five. Later in this chapter we'll suggest some specific things that you should try to accomplish during each visit. If you can spread them over a week, so much the better.

....

If you're harboring any doubts about moving to a small town, consider a longer stay or multiple visits. Use Rule 2:

Allow enough time.

Q: What if I decide right on the spot that the first town I visit is the perfect one?

A: If you're certain within the first half-hour of arriving in a town that "this is it, this is the one," that's great. Still, we recommend that you resist acting on this decision on the spot. Allow yourself a little distance and a little time before finalizing it. We recommend you go ahead and visit the second most likely candidate on your shortlist just to verify your thinking about the first one.

Q: When should we make our visit?

A: Plan to visit when you can see the town during both a workday and a weekend, for example from Thursday to Sunday. You might want to visit each of your towns during the season in which you would expect less than perfect weather, especially if you have doubts whether you can tolerate the weather year-round. Avoid visiting a town during August, if you can, when many of the locals are away on vacation. Avoid major tourist events as well. You won't get a true feeling for the town if it's swarming with tourists for the annual Harvest Festival. (Or extend your visit for a couple of days before or after the event, so you'll have a chance to see the town at its normal pace.)

The ideal time to visit one of your shortlist towns may be quite different than for another. You might have to make some compromises as you plan your visits.

Things to Bring When You Visit Your Small Town	• Your research files • A still or video camera • Maps of the region • A spiral-bound notebook to use as a visit log • Any guidebooks or historical books about the region that currently interests you (more will be available there) • Picnic and maybe camping gear	• Tape or stapler • Binoculars

What to Do During Your Visits

Here are some specific exercises we suggest, to get the most out of each of your shortlist visits. Please remember that these are only starting points. There may be other projects that you need to carry out because of your individual situation.

Keep a Visit Log. This exercise is important. Before your visits, go out and buy a plain old spiral-bound notebook. Nothing fancy. Write the name of the town you will visit first at the top of the first page. Attach your Shortlist Worksheet for that town on the inside front cover, so you can research and amend it on-site. When you get there, write notes on your feelings, reactions, and instincts about the place. If you're making the trip with others, aggressively solicit log entries at least once a day. *(Hey! Anybody got anything they want to put into the log?)* Get everybody into the act.

Bring tape or a stapler. If there's a real estate listing, a school lunch menu, or *anything* else that matters to any one of you, tape it in. Repeat this process for each town you visit. This will be a useful reference when you choose your town later on.

Use Your Still or Video Camera. A visual record of where you've been and what you've done can be helpful. If you're visiting four or five towns, they may tend to blur together a little after you get home. Take pictures or videos of the best—and worst—aspects of each town. Make it fun. That way, when you make a final decision, you'll be sure that you're picking town A because of what you liked about town A, not something that was actually in town B or C.

Deputize the Investigators. Make sure that *everybody* has a job to do during a visit. Make sure everybody has a chance to participate. Deputize them; split up the information you are seeking and assign the appropriate person responsibility for finding it. This includes kids, if you have yours with you. You might have a deputy of senior centers (Grandma?), and a deputy of parks and playgrounds (your six-year-old?), and a deputy of real estate (your spouse?). It's even better if each person is deputized to find the same information in each different town you visit. That way for every major question you have there will be one person with a comprehensive view of all the shortlist towns.

Explore Beyond the Tourist Level. When we travel for fun, most of us travel like tourists to some degree. We eat in tourist places. We spend time on tourist activities. We act as if we are on vacation. Or, if we're traveling for work, we eat at restaurants that cater to business travelers, and we take cabs and flake out in front of the TV at night. That's fine, if the purpose of your trip is a vacation or business. In this case, it's not. Approach each visit as if you already live in that town. To the greatest extent possible, put yourself in the frame of mind of a local resident. For example, it's noon. You're hungry. Don't go to a fast-food chain outlet alongside the highway, go into town to a neighborhood deli or grocery store and buy sandwich makings. Have your sandwich on a park bench. That way you get several chances to talk with the locals. Also make reservations to stay at a locally-owned motel or bed-and-breakfast inn, preferably in the heart of town so you can walk to everything. Or, if you're traveling by RV or camping and the town has a locally owned RV park or campsite, stay there.

> ....
> **You have to look beyond the wonderful dream you have of what a small town is and look at the realities. Especially if you're coming out of an urban area.**
>
> —Liz P.

Schedule Part of Your Time. Figure out the most important questions or concerns you have, and allocate enough time to deal with them satisfactorily. Make certain that the critical concerns don't slip through the cracks. Open your visit log each morning and write out a schedule for the day that includes these critical missions and who is going on them.

Keep Part of Your Time Unscheduled. Make sure you leave a few good-sized blocks of free time in your schedule. Allow for serendipity. You may get into a town and discover something completely unexpected and wonderful. You may get invited to dinner at a new friend's house. (That sort of thing actually happens in small towns.) It would be a shame not to be able to enjoy it because your schedule is too full.

Use Your Network. Through your research you have almost certainly had some phone or mail contact with people in each of your shortlist towns. There may have been a few who were particularly friendly and helpful. Before your visit, call them up and tell them you're coming to visit. Ask if you can drop by to meet them. Invite them out for coffee. You may just want to say thanks for their help, or you may have additional questions. They will be pleased to meet you and show off their little town.

Visit Your Employment Contacts. You may be going on a job interview or two; there are some other contacts you might want to make as well. Stop by to introduce yourself to the person you had those phone conversations with, such as at the Chamber of Commerce. Go meet the people who you might end up doing business with, or those who might be your competition.

Take Each Commute for a Test Drive. One of you will probably be working at a job in your new small town. If so, in each shortlist town you visit, simulate a typical commute. At "rush hour" some afternoon, drive from a place where you could see yourself working to a place where you could see yourself living.

Just to make it a fair test, pick the potential workplace and the potential neighborhood that are farthest from each other. That way you'll know what your worst-case commute would be. Time the trip. Count the number of stoplights. Record it in your visit log. If you are the urban survivor of interminable bumper-to-bumper commutes, we suspect that this exercise alone will erase any lingering doubts you might have about moving to a small town.

Do you think you might like to have the option of walking to work? If so, walk a commute route in each town you visit. Time your walk. Record it in your visit log. If you enjoy walking, you might want to track which town has the most pleasant routes to likely destinations.

Are the buildings and grounds well maintained?	**What to Look**
How large is the typical class size?	**for When You**
Are the students polite and friendly to each other?	**Visit a School**
Are there graffiti?	
Is there adequate evidence of adult supervision?	
Is the curriculum up to date and to your liking?	
Do the students walk to school? Ride bikes? Or, if old enough, do they drive?	
How do the teachers handle the students? Is the atmosphere friendly but firm? Permissive? Rigidly strict?	
Are there quiet places for the students to study? If so, are they being used?	
Are there after-school activities? Have extracurricular activities been cut because of budget restraints?	
Does the community use the school facilities for evening classes or other organized activities?	
Do you see any parent volunteers working with students?	

Visit the Schools. If you have kids, this is an important exercise. Most schools are happy to accommodate visit requests. Besides the myriad questions you'll look into at every likely school, check whether the specific statistical data you collected is accurate. Chat with the teachers, princi-pal, and students. Ask any questions that occur to you as a result of your visit.

You may need to take your kids out of their current schools in order for them to visit your candidate small towns. While no parent likes to do this more than necessary, the benefit of school-year visits is that your kids can check out the schools in person. This usually can be arranged with local school administrators. Just explain that you are considering a move to their school district and you'd like to let your kids take the local school for a short test drive. They may be willing to assign each child a "buddy" to show them around for a day.

We'll warn you right now that the hardest part of this exercise is selling your kids on the concept of attending an unfamiliar school while they are on what seems to them like a vacation. Tell them it's worth it. Tell them there'll be no homework, no tests. Then tell them it's the only way they can find out which schools are cool and which are full of geeks. After that, they'll go. Be sure to log your observations and theirs.

Visit Organizations of Interest to You. Don't be shy. Check the local paper and see what's going on. Is the local volunteer fire department hold-ing a pancake breakfast fund-raiser? Is there a show by the local quilting society? Are the members of the spelunking club holding a slide show? Join in. You'll be able to meet people, ask questions, and make friends.

Take a Walking Tour of Each Town	
	• Walk up and down the main streets. Take a look at the businesses. Get a sense of the health of the place. Are there empty storefronts? Many?
	• Find an old neighborhood and walk through it. Are the houses well main-tained, or are they deteriorating?
	• Walk through a newer neighborhood. What is it like? How will it look in ten years?
	• Walk through an industrial/commercial area. Are most of the commercial properties kept passably neat, or does it look like a region of junkyards?

Walk. Using a process called *walking* you can actually cover surprising distances. We've taught ourselves to do it.

When you visit your shortlist towns, walk everywhere you can. True, it's slower, but you can actually see things, and you'll meet people. You'll notice things about a small town that you never would from a car. And, yes, it gives you a feel for the place.

Here are some suggestions for investigating real estate when you visit a town. Start by finding a neighborhood that seems like it's in your price range and might be one you'd like to live in. Sometimes the best way is to just walk through the neighborhoods and strike up a conversation with the people you encounter. There are some questions to answer:

- How is it zoned? What is the minimum lot size? Does it seem like the zoning regulations are enforced?
- Is it on a municipal sewer system, or do the residents use septic systems?
- Where does the tap water come from? A well? A lake? A reservoir? How good is it?
- How are most of the houses heated? Gas? Electric? Wood?
- Do many of the houses have air conditioning?
- Are there sidewalks?
- Where is the nearest fire station?
- Are there fire hydrants or must fires be fought using tank trucks?
- Are the streets in good repair?
- How are the houses maintained? Are they well kept up? Are the yards neat?
- Are there signs of imminent development or other changes nearby?

Do a Housing Check. If you have not done so already you'll probably want to establish a relationship with a realtor in each of your shortlist towns, even if you're not planning to buy right away. A good realtor knows as much as anybody about local climate, zoning, schools, and a thousand other not-so-little details, and personally knows much of the populace. The relationship itself can be valuable to you; when you're ready to buy a house or rent a place, you'll know who to turn to for help.

If you are planning to buy, ask the realtor for a recent listing of houses and properties that are for sale in the area. Go look at some in your price range. It's not enough to look through the listings, you need to actually look at some real estate, whether you plan to rent an apartment or buy forty acres of pasture. Otherwise you might find out too late that the type of apartment or size of house or kind of land you want can only be found in an area that you don't like.

While you visit as many of your shortlist towns as you can, remember to pay attention to the soft data. Hold off acting on your choice until you've completed your visits and are back in your own living room. It could save you from making a big and costly mistake.

By the end of your visits you should have strong feelings, pro or con, about each of the small towns you have visited. The next chapter, where you'll choose a town based on those feelings, will be short and exciting.

CHAPTER 11

It's Time to Choose
Your New Town

You're back home now, after visiting the towns on your shortlist. You probably were disappointed by one or two of the towns you saw but found a couple to be as good as or better than you expected. Perhaps one or two were really exceptional. If there's only one possible town for you, skip right on to the next chapter and begin your move. If you are plagued by indecision, this chapter offers suggestions for moving toward a decision. If your group interests are divided, you'll also find suggestions here for uniting them in a decision. Reaching a decision you're happy to live with is the goal, regardless of your decision-making style.

The process of choice is different for every individual and for every family. Here are a few of the dozens of possible approaches to decision making:

Decision Making for Individuals

Talk Your Friends to Death. Consult with everybody you know about all possible variants, every advantage and disadvantage, every possible outcome until even close friends immediately change the subject. This will help you accumulate a variety of perspectives, but it may also delay a decision that ultimately is yours.

Just Do It. For the risk taker who is comfortable acting largely on impulse, there need not be a lot of talk. Continual excitement and readiness to embrace change support the modus operandi. This is a decisive approach, but be careful not to let impatience land you in a less than optimal town.

Use Your Intuition. Trust your instincts to guide you in making this important decision. Clear your head, go someplace quiet, and let your right brain ponder which town has the strongest pull.

Procrastinate Until Fate Decides. If you wait long enough, the decision on where to move may be made for you. You can procrastinate until you're forced to relocate because your lease runs out and the new rent is prohibitively expensive, or until a possible job transfer forces the issue, or until a new baby is on the way and you're still stuck in a tiny studio apartment. Procrastinating is not a recommended approach because it reduces the control and input you'll have; however, sometimes a major catalyst is what it takes to push life forward.

Decision Making for Families

In group decision making the same individual styles may appear, but there are more issues at stake and more opinions, feelings, and ideas involved. Most families have a hierarchy that has to be taken into account. Here are a few possible approaches:

Let the Head of Household Choose. This style is a modern twist on the traditional father-knows-best one. The head of household (these days that might be the father or the mother) makes the ultimate decision. Ideally, he or she takes everyone's feelings and thoughts into account, and a fair decision is made for the good of the whole family. There are always the more autocratic decision makers, however, who will lay down ultimatums that leave little room for anyone else's opinions. This can undo much of the group's consensus-building efforts.

Do as Jefferson Did. After much discussion, debate, and deliberation, take a democratic vote. The majority decision automatically passes.

Use an Outside Mediator. Invite wise Aunt Lulu over to advise, counsel, and mediate. Perhaps she can get everybody to at least listen to each other. If she's a real magician, she'll get everyone to agree. The downside of this approach is that you may end up living in Aunt Lulu's favorite town, which may not be the best town for your group.

Eliminate the Rotten Apples. Using this approach, it's not the best option that is chosen, it's the least flawed. If this is your group's style, consider each option fully and determine which town is least rotten. This one will be your best option. We don't wholeheartedly recommend this approach because it focuses on the negative rather than positive elements of a town.

**Special
Instructions:
If One Person
Must Make the
Decision for
Everybody Else**

For employment, health, or any of a thousand other reasons, only one person may make the choice of a new town for a whole family. If a family decision can't be democratic, we suggest that the person who makes the decision be sensitive to its impact. It is critical to explain the decision as fully as possible. The better everybody understands the decision, the more easily they will adapt to it.

Each of these styles differs from the others, yet each can work. That's all that really matters. The town that suits you and yours will be unique; so will the way in which you choose it. We'll tell you what worked for us, then suggest steps to arrive at a decision of your own.

**What's Our Bias?
Consensus**

We admit it right up front: We definitely have a bias when it comes to the best way of making a group decision. To the extent that it's possible, reach a workable consensus within your family, and base your decision on that consensus. From what we've seen, the people who base their choice of where to move on a workable group consensus seem to get the most out of their new towns.

The Process of Making a Decision

The decision-making styles above do have one thing in common; each represents a familiar if sometimes unconscious process. Very few of us are endowed with the ability to make instant decisions—especially when they involve major changes. Many of us can barely decide what to wear in the morning, which friends to have over on the weekend, or what to cook for dinner. So especially for major decisions, we develop a process. We examine the pros and cons of our options, we talk with others to get their input, we make comparisons to previous situations. We peer hard into our crystal balls, trying to get some sense of what lies ahead on each of several paths.

Indecision often results when we are fearful of the possible outcomes of a decision. In the case of making a move, your decision of where to go will affect your life and your family's, on many levels. There will be tangible outcomes, such as changes in your financial, employment, and housing status. There will also be intangible outcomes, such as happiness, relief, or loneliness. It's helpful to take a look at what your fears stem from. The more you have a feel for the positive and negative outcomes that might result from your decision, the easier it becomes to make a confident choice.

If you have a terrible time making decisions, try the following:

For the Decisionally Dysfunctional

1. Give yourself time and space to think through your options. Indecision can often result from being overstressed.
2. Gather solid information on which to base your decisions. The more informed you are, the more confident you will be in making a decision.
3. Listen to your instincts. Sometimes we listen so much to what others think we should do that we forget to listen to ourselves.
4. Chart a course. Take extra time to explore your unique needs and desires. If these change frequently, see if you can define at least a general direction for yourself, and work from there.
5. Set a firm, but not rushed, decision deadline.

At the beginning of our search for a small town, we suffered from decision paralysis. A lack of clear direction was the most obvious reason. Neither one of us was sure where we were headed with our careers. But there was a more subtle reason too; we had quite different views on what we wanted in a small town. Our lively discussions focused on trying to convince each other of our own right kind of town. Since our "right" kinds were dissimilar, this was bound to result in conflict. After awhile we simply avoided the subject altogether. The only thing we seemed to agree on was to make no decision at all.

Fortunately, our paralysis had an end. After making a concerted effort to get a little better at team decision making, we arrived at more productive ways of reaching a decision together. The rest of this chapter is devoted to useful techniques for forming consensus with others about where to move. Use what you find helpful and disregard the rest.

> **The sooner you do it, the sooner everything will start falling into place. The longer you wait for the right moment, the harder it will be to make a move.**
>
> – Dave F.

A Special Note to Singles

If you are the only one who will be moving to a small town, your decision-making process will be simpler than if you are moving not only yourself but your five kids, a spouse, your mother, your father-in-law, a hamster, and two Great Danes. The single person will only have to reach consensus with himself or herself. However, this is not necessarily an automatic process. Much of the information here is useful to those moving alone as well.

Reaching Consensus

Reaching consensus within a group takes time, often a lot of talking, and tolerance while you explore any conflicts. The following steps to group decisions may ease you over a few of the hurdles and rough spots.

You may also want to refer to the explanation of the seven rules in Chapter 4, as a refresher.

Now, take a deep breath and dive in. In a few hours or days you'll have picked your new town.

Put Your Thumb on the Scale	Put all the data and quantitative information about a town on one side of a scale. Then put your heart—your feelings about the place—on the other side of the scale. Press very lightly with your thumb on the side of the scale holding your heart. Then decide.

○ **Decision Step 1: Call a Decision Conference**

> ....
>
> **If your deliberations repeatedly return to what's wrong instead of right in your choices, you may be getting too tired to give this decision your best. Hold to Rule 1:** *Seek a positive trait instead of avoiding a negative one.*

Get everybody who will be moving to your new town together for a conference. That means everybody. Whether or not they went on the visits to your shortlist towns, they should be here. Whether or not they've started kindergarten, they should be here. Everybody. The purpose of the meeting is to choose which small town *all* of you will soon call home.

Obviously, if you are moving alone, the chances of achieving 100 percent attendance at this conference will be very good. Still, schedule a meeting with yourself just as you would with somebody else. It will help you to approach the decision with a clear mind, and support taking whatever time you need.

○ **Decision Step 2: Take a "Favorites" Poll**

Go around the room giving everybody a chance to name a choice and to state in detail why it is the favorite. If you are running the meeting, hold off any discussion for the time being. Just go around the room and let everybody have a say without interruption. This is the time for everybody to listen to each other, a chance for everybody to voice opinions, not the final say.

| **Allow for Town Shrinkage** | Virtually everybody we have spoken with who has moved to a small town has described a phenomenon we have come to refer to as *town shrinkage*. That is to say, after a year or two every one of them swore that they woke up one morning and realized their town had shrunk the night before. Some towns shrank by 20 percent, a few by 50 percent. But they all seemed to shrink a little.

This is just something to be aware of as you decide. A town that feels a little large right now may feel just right after a couple years. A town that already feels a little small may feel even smaller in a few years. |
| --- | --- |

Did everybody come up with the same town? If so, wonderful.
Go straight to Decision Step 5.

What if all of you came up with different favorite towns? Well, you
have a little work to do. Don't give up hope. Compromise leads to consensus.

○ **Decision Step 3: Take a "Runner-Up" Poll**

If you know you're *really* close to a choice, if all of you seem to
be transmitting on almost the same wavelength, then get your nose out
of this book, keep talking, and make your decision. If you're that close,
don't let up. When you decide, go directly to Step 5 and celebrate.

But if you're not quite that close, do this: Ask everybody what
their second choice is and why. Go around the room as in Decision Step 2,
asking the name of everybody's runner-up choice and, in detail, why.
Just as before, give everybody a chance to speak without interruption
or contradiction.

Did a particular runner-up town emerge as a strong contender?
Is this a town around which you might be able to form consensus? Explore
whether this is the best town for the needs of the group as a whole.
If another poll confirms that it is, this is your exit to Decision Step 5.

If not, try Decision Step 4.

○ **Decision Step 4: Forge a "Workable" Consensus**

Maybe you're pursuing perfect consensus when what you can use
is workable consensus. What's the difference?

A perfect consensus leaves everybody saying, *This small town
couldn't be any better.* A workable consensus leaves everybody saying,
*It's not absolutely ideal, but this small town is a whole world better than
where we live now.* Of course you want a perfect consensus. But if that's
not possible, a workable consensus may be in order.

Each of you should answer two fundamental questions about the
small towns you are considering, as a way to finding grounds for workable consensus: Can I see myself being happy there? Can I see everybody else being happy there?

This choice is an issue of the heart, not of the head. To the greatest
extent possible, make sure that each person understands the reasons for
each other's preferences and the feelings as well. Go into detail. Again,
anyone who feels they have been ignored or been steamrolled into a
decision that they simply do not want to accept will likely be a source of
resistance in the future. It is much better to listen fully at this point and
accommodate to the extent that you can. Keep on trying.

Don't give anybody
a hard time for
following Rule 6:
*Change your mind
whenever you need to.*

Even if the feelings
aren't clear—and if
they're not, try to
clarify them non-
judgmental—they
matter. Apply Rule 3:
*Feelings are as
important as facts.*

Focus on discussion, rather than on trying to convince each other of a point of view. Make only your formal polls the decision points, and the rest of the time just talk to clarify your opinions and feelings. By asking questions, listening with an open mind, and working together to examine the pros and cons of a place, you can help each other come to a decision. If you feel you're getting closer to a final choice, keep discussing. Are you stalled? Keep discussing. By now, you either have a decision or you can't talk anymore.

Break the Indecision Log Jam

Are you experiencing an epidemic of indecision? Step back and take a look at the dynamics of your situation:

- Is there one person in your group who seems particularly dubious about moving to a small town? Are these doubts playing on everyone's worst fears? Try talking to this person, either in the group or separately, about his or her feelings. Get a better understanding of the doubts and whether there is anything that can be done to lessen them.
- Are you and your partner perhaps in greater disagreement than you realize? Are you avoiding a final decision in order to avoid conflict? Discuss openly what is going on and how you can approach decision making in a more productive way.
- Are you the primary decision maker in your family and feeling seriously uncomfortable about taking responsibility for such a major one? Try increasing the involvement of the rest of the family in the decision-making process even if you have to backtrack to do it.
- Are you and others in your group paralyzed by fear of the unknown? Take extra steps to familiarize yourself with the small towns on your finalist list. The more you get to know about them—and how you feel about them—the easier it will be to make a decision.

If each of you is holding out for your own perfect solution, and none of you is willing to compromise, accommodate, rethink, or otherwise bend, then all of you will find yourselves stuck at your present address. Did you really come this far only to run into a brick wall of your own making? Of course not. So don't give up. Try the following technique.

If you can't agree on which of the serious contenders you like best, maybe you can agree on which one you like least, and eliminate it. At least you will narrow the field by one. Go ahead, try it. It will feel good to agree on *something*. Now, try it again. Knock another one off the list, and soon you'll sneak up on a choice from behind. The bottom line is to do whatever seems to work.

If you're reading this, you must be in deep mud. Get a copy of the book *Getting to Yes* by Roger Fisher and William Ury, the negotiator's bible. Put your discussions on hold. Skim through it. See what parts of it pertain to the impasses you are facing. Use their techniques; diplomats and union leaders have. Then try again.

You could also try calling time out. Consider dropping the whole subject for a week or a month. Time may allow passions to cool and flexibility to return. When you approach the choice again, use your imagination. Be patient with each other. Maintain a sense of humor. And above all, be persistent. You'll get there. Good luck.

○ **Decision Step 5: Make Your Choice Official**

It's a good idea to make your choice official as soon as you can. Right now is a perfectly good time. After all, there are a lot of final arrangements that have to be made: moving vans, realtors, jobs, taxes. Before you start arranging your move, you want to reinforce having everybody on the same train headed for the same destination. Go get some champagne or make some popcorn or order Chinese take-out, whatever you do to celebrate good news. Have a "we finally picked a new small town!" party. Congratulate yourself and each other. You've earned it.

We're going to help you move. Really, we will. Yeah . . . we know, friends always say that. But in the next chapter we'll help you plan the move that will work best for you. And in the chapter after that, we'll provide some techniques for settling smoothly into your new town.

three

Making the Move
Right

SECTION THREE

CHAPTER 12

Strategies for Your Move

All along we've been saying that you—and only you—know what is best for you. It was true when you were trying to figure out which town to choose, and it's just as true while you plan how you are going to make the transition to life in a small community. You may feel you've just found the best little town on either side of the Great Divide, but figuring out how to get there could look a little overwhelming. This chapter focuses on the means to a smooth logistical and emotional transition to your new town. This is no time for extra potholes and bumps.

Change Is Risky

Let's be honest. Making the transition to a new town involves risk. There is a risk that after a year you won't like the place. There is a risk that you won't like the people or they won't like you. You might not make enough money. Your kids could hate it. The house you buy could lose value. We're not trying to scare you; with all your research, you've done everything possible to anticipate and avoid such risks. But your threshold for and style of managing the risk that does exist is an important consideration in planning the speed and logistics of your move, and also your housing, employment, and other arrangements once there.

Where Are Your Risk Thresholds?

People are funny about risk; they are not consistent. A person may be willing to accept huge risks in some areas of life and virtually no risk in other areas. Take for an example a woman who puts a parachute on her back and spends every free weekend jumping out of perfectly good airplanes while a mile above the earth, yet handles her money with extreme caution. Physically, she is *risk inclined*. Financially, she is *risk averse*. She probably doesn't feel that she's inconsistent at all. In fact, this sky-diving financial bear would probably classify both activities as neither risky nor cautious but perfectly reasonable.

If a group of you are moving together, you may have to accommodate risk thresholds that feel quite foreign. Though the other people may seem quite inconsistent to you, they themselves probably don't feel that they are inconsistent at all. Even if you are moving alone the inconsistencies you see—in yourself—may surprise you. That's OK. If you have to choose between doing the consistent thing and doing the best thing, do the best thing.

So, how do you feel about risk? Honestly. Are you risk inclined? Risk averse? And about what? Are you willing to take more risk yourself than you are willing to impose on your family? With money are you inherently cautious, or do you have an *in for a penny—in for a pound* attitude? These are among the types of questions you'll need to consider as you plan your transition. There are no right or wrong answers to shoot for, only answers honest enough to help you make good decisions when planning the details of your move.

Risk Inclined	Risk Averse	How Much of a Risk Taker Are You?
Blind date with tattoo artist	Steady date with dental hygienist	
Entrepreneurism	Staff employment	
Escargots	Oatmeal	
Stock options	Treasury bills	
Rollerblading	Lawn bowling	
Blackjack	Bingo	
Karaoke at a nightclub	Singing in the shower	
Harley Davidson	Minivan	
Windsurfing	Shell collecting	

O **Mind Merge**

If you're moving with others block out some time to discuss each other's threshold for risk, especially in strategies for the move, housing, and finance. (We'll list elements to consider in a moment.) You may not be aware of how much anxiety a change—even a good change— can cause in one of your children or in your spouse. If there are widely varying levels of comfort with change, take time to find an approach that works for everyone. For example, if you're a fly-by-the-seat-of-the-pants type and the person you're moving with is a plan-every-detail-into-the-ground type, you can avoid a lot of stress and conflicts by agreeing up front on a moving strategy that works for both of you. You might take responsibility for the move itself, which may well have unexpected twists requiring fast decisions, while your partner makes the more permanent arrangements for once you're there.

The key is to communicate. Ask the others in your group how they'd prefer to organize the move. Tell them your thoughts on the subject. Above all, listen carefully to each other. What will get you from your current situation to your new town with the least anxiety and most comfort?

What to Consider When Planning Your Moving Strategy

Moving is not the sort of thing people do for fun. In fact, most people would put moving on par with knee surgery or an IRS audit. There are dozens of decisions to make, details to figure out, unexpected upsets to somehow figure in, and there are many, many boxes to lift. Figuring out an overall approach and moving strategy *before* you get into the thick of the logistical details will help you get through your move more smoothly.

Moving strategies are not limited to just a few choices. There are dozens of variations. For example, you can choose risk-inclined options concerning real estate, risk-neutral options in moving dates, and risk-averse options for starting a business. (That's what we did.) Taking a risk-averse option in one area doesn't mean that all of the rest of your choices also have to be risk averse. Being a financial conservative shouldn't stop you from being a weekend skydiver.

The following list of questions, considerations, and possible solutions will get you started.

Level of Commitment. Should you dive into your new town all at once, or should you ease in over time? The answer depends greatly on your risk threshold and how confident you feel about the new town you've chosen. It also depends on how anxious you are to leave your current situation.

You might:
- make a clean break and move everything to your new town right away
- spend a summer there first to check it out
- if moving with others, send one ahead of the rest to scout things out for a month or two
- spend most weekends there for several months, and move gradually
- arrange to take a leave and try it out for a year

Housing. Most housing issues are logistical. However, if you've been living in the same place for years, are considering selling a house that's been in the family for generations, or have other strong attachments, there will be emotional issues to handle as well. Here are several logistical issues that you'll need to consider:

What do you do about your current residence? Whether you rent or own, you might:

- sublease your current apartment or rent out your current house, until you're sure you've made the right move
- give up your apartment or sell your house as soon as you can
- lease your current house with a buy option, if you're having trouble selling it

What do you do about all of your stuff? You could:

- move it all now
- store it for awhile and just move the necessities for now

What do you do about a new residence? You might:

- rent month to month, perhaps while you scout out the perfect house or build a new one
- sign a one-year lease
- buy right away because the local housing market is going up quickly

---

A Two-Step Housing Solution

For us, the best housing choice seemed to be a fairly conservative one. Ultimately, we want to find a dream piece of property and build a house. But for a while that would be beyond our means. Also, we knew of people who had bought property within months of their move and who admitted a few years later they would have bought a different piece of property had they known the region better. We wanted to avoid that pitfall. We wanted to invest in some property, so we found a smaller house that we knew we could sell easily or use later as rental property. It isn't exactly our style, but it's proven to be an excellent interim solution.

Finances. How do you arrange your financial and employment situation? This is often the most difficult issue that comes up. If you're moving with a partner, finding a solution that fits both of your needs can be a challenge. It's important to take into consideration everyone's comfort level with risk so you can minimize any stress and anxiety.

You might:

- stay put until you have a fall-back cushion saved in the bank
- move immediately without any financial cushion

You also might:

- quit your job outright

- make arrangements to take a leave of absence
- move to your new town and then find a job
- make sure you have a job lined up in your new town before you move
- buy an existing, proven business in your new town
- move first and dive into a new business when you get there

Timing. What is the best time to move? Timing can greatly affect how smooth your transition is. For example, moving into a new place in a freezing cold rain can put a real damper on your excitement and cause damage to your belongings. Changing schools in midyear can cause a lot of added anxiety for your children. Trying to sell your house at the wrong time of year can compound the logistical challenge. You may not have a lot of control over deciding when you move. But if you do, consider what would be the best time to:

- leave your current employment
- put your current house on the market
- buy or rent a place in your new town
- start a business
- get the kids settled into school
- avoid bad weather

Moving Logistics. Many good books are available on how best to plan your moving logistics. Most moving companies will provide you with pamphlets, checklists, videos, and even comic books for your children. To get started, you might:

- Figure out the cost difference between renting a truck and hiring a moving company. Don't forget to factor in such sometimes hidden considerations as your own time and possible personal injury risk if you move the stuff yourself.
- Find out if your moving expenses are tax deductible and, if so, what type of records you have to keep.
- If you decide to use a moving company, contact several to get bids and find out if they will guarantee you a fixed rate.
- Set aside some extra time to sort and toss. Moving is a great opportunity to lighten your load of dust-gathering household goods. Consider holding a moving sale or donating unwanted items to your local charity.

Moving with Kids and Dependents

At dinner a few months before we moved, we had (and lost) the standard *at-least-you-have-to-try-them* argument about brussels sprouts with our six-year-old son. We jokingly told him that brussels sprouts were the only food that was available where we were moving. Everything was made from brussels sprouts. Breakfast cereal. Ice cream. Everything. He responded with a silent frown. We assumed he knew we were joking and we forgot the whole matter.

Several months later, the week before our move, our son dug in his heels and emphatically voiced his decision to stay put. No way was he going to move. Finally it came out: He *hated* brussels sprouts and had no intention of moving to a place where he would have to eat them all the time. We remembered our joke. It had backfired. After many reassurances and a promise that we'd turn the moving van around if he didn't find anything more than brussels sprouts in the grocery store, he agreed to at least try the new place. He loves it here now.

Moving is an emotional and stressful time, even if it's a smooth move to a wonderful place. Moving with kids and elderly dependents can add to the stress if extra consideration to their needs and feelings isn't provided. Rule 3 is particularly important: *Feelings are as important as facts.* Many children and elderly persons are creatures of habit. They have their routines and they are often quite cautious about change. A move to a small town is about as big a disruption of their world as they could imagine. They may be excited about the change—but scared at the same time. A little sensitivity and flexibility now may avoid a lot of adaptation anxiety later.

What can you do to make the transition as easy as possible for your kids and elderly dependents? Communication and planning ahead are crucial. Here are a few suggestions:

- Convene weekly or even daily briefings, to make sure everyone is fully aware of what's going on and when.
- Include everyone in your planning as much as you can.
- Figure out a way to involve everyone in the move by assigning each one a useful role.
- Meet with your elderly parent's health-care provider to discuss how to make the transition to a new place easy and smooth.
- Plan a special good-bye event with your child's day-care provider or teacher.
- Arrange a special event so your elderly parent can say good-bye to friends.

....

If your teenagers are addicted to malls, they're going to have a heck of a time adjusting to the country. When my stepdaughter came to visit us, she burst into tears because we were eighteen miles from the nearest mall.

— Liz P.

Use Your Left Brain to Design the Logistics

In the Introduction we mentioned the saying *what you get is how you do it*, referring to how greatly your end result (life in a new town) will be influenced by how you achieve it (the manner of your search for, choice of, and move to your new home). In other words, you will find it much easier to segue into a new life if your moving process is well organized, unharried, and low key. Use these means of keeping track:

- For each discrete critical task, establish a deadline so no one is running around at the last minute.
- Put up a checklist on the your former research bulletin board, so everyone can see what's been accomplished and what still needs to be done.
- Put up a calendar on your bulletin board, too, so you can mark off the days until you move to your new town.

○ **Mind Merge**

Once you think you have a general idea of how and when you'll move, get everybody together and start to spell it out in detail. Make sure everybody understands the plan. Ask if there are any suggestions. Make sure that your plan takes everybody's needs into account. If not, make the changes that are necessary. Moving is never easy, but a little planning and consideration can greatly reduce the inconvenience for everybody.

○ **Reality Check**

Before you finalize your moving plans, step back and take a look at them. Are you allowing enough time? Do you have enough money set aside to pay for the move? Do you have a bit of a financial buffer in case something goes wrong during the move? Has anything happened since you started to plan your move that makes you think you should modify some part of your plans? If so, take this time to adapt to changed realities.

Use Your Right Brain to Smooth Your Move

When planning a move, it is very easy to be ruled by the left brain. Moving is an exercise in logistics, after all. What must be done first, before other things can be done? What is the cheapest way to move? What is the fastest cheap way? These questions are exactly what your left brain was designed for. But be careful. You are likely to have problems if you defer to it totally.

Your right brain deserves a say. You may be very happy to be leaving your present home. You may be certain that your new home is close to perfect. Still, there may be some things that you regret leaving behind. Set aside an evening for a last dinner at that Chinese restaurant you like so much. Go for a last walk in the park near your house.

Allow plenty of time to say good-bye. You will be leaving a circle of friends and perhaps family. You may be certain that most of them will come visit you in your new home, and you may even be betting that a few will move to join you within a few years. But still, your move to a new town marks the end of one era in your life and the beginning of another. The more you allow yourself to enjoy the end of this era of your life, the more you'll enjoy the beginning of the next one.

The next chapter addresses this new life you're beginning. It draws on the experience of other émigrés to suggest how to settle quickly and comfortably into your new town.

CHAPTER 13

Settling In

The purpose of this chapter is to help you get the most out of your move to a new town. Think of it as trying to get the most out of a harvest.

There are two parts to a successful harvest. First, you plant high-quality seeds and use an efficient growing method. Second, you waste very little as you put your crop to use. You've already done the first part. You've already found a town that's close to perfect for you. The way in which you settle into your new town will determine how much reward you get from your efforts.

Small towns look different on the outside because they are different on the inside. In order to reap the greatest possible benefit from your new town, you will probably end up living your day-to-day life differently than you now do. Living in a small town is likely to demand some internal changes, as well.

What follows are suggestions for settling smoothly into your new life.

Pace Yourself. A mistake city folk tend to make when first arriving in a small town is to think a slower pace means less productivity. It doesn't. This reaction is typical, though. In an urban environment, often the only way to accomplish anything is to maintain a frenetic pace. When the pace is slow and unhurried, we automatically assume that nothing is getting done. Not necessarily true. If you remove the urban environment—traffic, parking, crowds—you also remove a lot of the elements that forced you to be frenetic in the first place. With those things out of the way, you can be productive without being frenetic. Nice thought. Welcome to small towns.

How does this affect you as you settle in? If you're anything like us, you will have to deliberately put on the brakes at first. It will take some effort.

....

Eighty percent of my conversations with people the first few months were: where did I come from, what did I do, and how long was I going to be here. People want to know if you're here to stay.

—Kesho S.

Let's say you've been in town a month. You're waiting in line at the hardware store, and the guy in front of you starts to talk with the clerk about firewood. And he goes on, and on, and on. And you're tapping your foot. Your "one-month-in-a-small-town" reaction might be to tap your foot and express something like this, at least to yourself: *Hey c'mon pal, hurry it up will ya? Cuz I got places to be and things to do and people to see OK and I gotta whole buncha stuff I gotta get done now OK so I don't have time to waste listening to you run on and on and on about who has the best firewood and who stacks it neatest so willya pleeze pay the guy and move on so I can get going now PLEEZE!*

This will change over time. Your "one-year-in-a-small-town" reaction might be to tap the shoulder of the guy in front of you and say, *Hey Fred, who'd you say is selling wood?*

Here's what we suggest: Skip right over your "one-month-in-a-small-town" phase. This will take conscious effort, but do your best to deliberately leave the frenetic urban pace behind from the start. Just hop right over it. Go right into your "one-year-in-a-small-town" phase. A large part of why you moved to a small town was the calmer pace, right? If so, you might as well slow yourself down from day one.

If you're coming from an urban environment, you're probably used to making a formal appointment to get information or take care of business. In many cases it isn't necessary in a small town. Sometimes you get more done simply by dropping by to do your business and taking time to chat with the people you encounter. This usually is just as productive. It's always a lot less harried. And it's a great way to get to know your new community, and to learn the useful bits and pieces of local information that will help you truly feel at home in your new town.

After a few months of living in a small town, you will realize that even though your pace has slowed significantly, your productivity is as high as or even higher than it was in the city. You'll be doing as much as before without having to be frenetic in order to get it done.

Adopt a Smaller, Healthier Attitude. You will not be anonymous in a small town. Though it may seem obvious, this fact is lost on many people when they first move. It was on us. A city dweller enjoys a certain dubious liberty that a small-town resident doesn't: If you act like a jerk in the city, you're just one more anonymous jerk among millions. In large cities, it's a survival tactic. Sometimes you've got to be a jerk just to get things done, right? Not so in small towns.

....
It's unrealistic if you think you're going to take your big city job experience and your university degrees and go to a small town and kick butt.

—Mac L.

You'll find fewer incompetents, lethargic slugs, and charter members of the Association of the Walking Brain Dead than you did in the city, but they'll be every bit as irritating. The one difference is that in the city it's almost guaranteed you will never come into contact with the same people twice. In a small town it's almost guaranteed that you will. So if you've treated them like a jerk, no matter how much they may have earned the honor, it will come back to haunt you.

Most urbanites readily acknowledge that tolerance and patience are virtues rapidly vanishing from their landscape. By comparison, the virtues are alive and well in small-town America. There is a simple reason for this. Without healthy amounts of tolerance, patience, and civility, a smaller community will not work in the first place. Be civil—as if you expect the favor to be returned. It will be.

| First Impressions Can Be Misleading | Outward signs of status are often less prominent in small towns than in urban areas; appearances can be deceiving. In rural areas, the wealthiest landowner may drive an old pickup truck, and that unshaven guy in ratty old jeans and work boots could turn out to be the county judge. |

....

When we built the house, we made a decision to use local labor as opposed to using contractors from out of town. We never even looked price-wise because it wouldn't have been a good way to intro-duce ourselves to a small town where everybody knows each other. Using local contractors helped us get through city planning and red tape because they had someone familiar to deal with.

—Bob M.

Remember, you're the new kid on the block, the one who will have to learn the local rules for freeze-tag and hide-and-seek. Be sensitive to the differences in pace, attitude, and custom. Make a conscious effort to adapt yourself to them.

Keep Your Money in the Community. This is important. A small town is a small economy. The decisions you make about where you spend your money will have a much bigger impact in a small town than they ever did in a city. Local small-town merchants depend on your dollars for their survival. Since there are fewer people in a small town than in a city, each of those merchants is that much more dependent on your business. They know it, too. The best service we've ever received has been from small-town merchants. You can contribute to the cycle of this responsiveness with your patronage, from the minute you start to unpack your moving van.

There's another benefit to buying locally. Your support of local mer-chants will not go unnoticed. It will be appreciated and it will open some doors for you into your new community. There's a strong ethic of reciprocity in many small towns. The *you scratch my back, I'll scratch yours* dynamic is alive and well. It holds especially if you are planning to run your own business in your new town. So buy locally, whenever possible.

Let's say you're planning to buy a piece of garden equipment. You already know that if you drive from your small town into the city you can buy it from one of those huge discount palaces for $100. Add 10 percent to the $100 city price; that's $110. Now, if you can find the same or a comparable piece of garden equipment for less than $110 from a local merchant, buy it. That way you've saved the gas, avoided a trip to the city or suburban mall, and supported a local merchant, all at once.

What happens if you find the piece of equipment locally but the price is more than $110? Go to the local store, tell them about your 10 percent rule, say you'd much rather spend your money locally, and then show them the city price. Ask if they can afford to meet your $110 price. If they can, they will. After all, they want your business. And you know you're probably going to get much better service after the sale from a local merchant than you ever would from one of those discount palaces fifty or a hundred miles down the road.

Adopt a 10 Percent Rule

Always Volunteer for Something. Everybody has seen one of those old black and white movies where the old soldier advises the new recruit, *Listen kid, just keep yer mouth shut and don't never volunteer fer nuthin'.* That old soldier never lived in a small town, which runs on volunteer labor: volunteer firefighters, public school volunteers, the sheriff's auxiliary, volunteer ambulance services, public library volunteers, and so on. Small towns are stoked by volunteers and couldn't function otherwise.

The town that we now live in, like many others, is too small to have a professional, full-time firefighting force. For the good of all, a handful of generous souls, Eric among them, volunteers to be on call twenty-four hours a day, seven days a week. For no more reward than a heartfelt thank you, they get up at any hour of the night and put themselves at personal risk to protect the lives and property of our neighbors.

One of the best ways to make friends in your new town is to volunteer. As soon as you unpack, start thinking about how you can put something into the pot. Look at your skills. Look at the needs in your small town. Then find a match. There's always a shortage of volunteers.

In a small town, you have more of a one-on-one contact with people in the business community. They treat you nicely because they want your business. If they don't treat you courteously, everyone in town knows by five o'clock.

— Kesho S.

Not sure where to start? Ask around. Also, most local phone books have listings of volunteer agencies. Check the headings "volunteer centers" and "clubs and organizations." Or contact these groups:

Library	Fire department
School district	Neighborhood school
Local hospital	Public health department
Social service agencies	Charity organizations

Volunteering in Your Community

Senior center   Youth center
Your church   Environmental organizations
Chamber of Commerce   Visitors center

Participate. In a small town, each individual's participation has an impact. If your influence changes the way 1,000 people in New York City vote in an election, it is unlikely that anybody will even notice. But if you change how 1,000 people vote in a town of 3,000, your impact is profound. The moral here is simple: Participation is your key to your new community.

The many opportunities for participation include elections, school assemblies, town meetings, and planning and development meetings. Take advantage of all that you can, becoming a part of your new community instead of merely being a recently arrived spectator on the sidelines. The more you participate, the more you'll feel like an integral and valued part of your new town.

Creating Your Community Niche

If there are no opportunities to get involved in your community in the way you'd like, create one. Here are a few ideas:

Form a political committee	Form a common interest group
Start a new community theater	Bring together a musical group
Initiate a planning committee	Initiate a recycling plan
Organize a special festival	Organize a sports event
Start a speakers series	Coordinate an issues debate
Coordinate children's services	Form a baby-sitting exchange
Form a book group	Start a discussion salon
Start a youth group	Organize a children's fair
Coordinate an art showing	Start a community art gallery
Do a fund-raising event	Organize a church bazaar
Start a bilingual program	Coordinate a local-history event

Know Your Local Government. In a small town, government is something you have to do for yourself. There is not the budget to support a lot of paid "professional" political people. In a small town, paid positions tend to be reserved for people who provide essential public safety services, such as police protection, firefighting, and public works.

We're not suggesting that you file for the next mayor's race as soon as you arrive in town. We are, however, suggesting that you make a conscious effort to get to know your government well enough to understand the local issues.

Pick one or two local issues that are of interest to you, and follow them as they evolve. Vote in every election. Go to several of the following meetings:

City council	County commission
City planning board	County planning board
School board	Social welfare commission

Local government entities may be known by different names in your new community. Find out the basics about them:

- When and where do they meet?
- How often are elections held?
- Which positions are appointed?
- Is fresh blood introduced from time to time, or has each seat been homesteaded in perpetuity by its occupant?
- What is the procedure for offering public testimony?

You will reap two benefits if you get to know your local government. First, you will be able to better understand the general forces at work in your community. This will give you a sense of your local history and trends in growth and development. Second, should the need arise, you will know how to respond to an issue that directly affects you. This could be important; urgent situations do come up that should be addressed.

We live on the edge of town. A few houses from us was a field with old oak trees and about the best blackberry bushes in the county. Within the space of several weeks, the owner had bulldozed the blackberries, cut down all the trees, and announced plans for a high-density development. We had problems with his plans. Traffic, fire safety, population density, and the impact on local schools were all issues that we felt had not been adequately addressed. Of course, we'd have preferred that the property remained a blackberry patch forever, but we knew that it would be developed eventually. We objected to the *type* of development he proposed.

Together with many others in the neighborhood, we fought his plans and stopped the high-density development. This involved offering public testimony before the city planning board, writing letters, and even locating and submitting an aerial photograph of the area in question. Had we not known how our local government functioned and who to contact, the chances are that we would now be the disgruntled neighbors of an inappropriately high-density housing development.

| **A Definition of Community** | Community is a dynamic whole that emerges when a group of people:
• participate in common practices;
• depend upon one another;
• make decisions together;
• identify themselves as part of something larger than the sum of their individual relationships; and
• commit themselves for the long term to their own, one another's, and the group's well-being.
From *Creating Community Anywhere,* by Carolyn Shaffer and Kristin Anundsen |

Consciously Creating Community

In your new town you'll have the opportunity to be a part of a real community. The satisfaction of connecting to those around you and to a group at large doesn't happen spontaneously. It takes time and effort. You'll need to take some conscious and deliberate steps to get involved. The actions discussed above—taking time for people, volunteering, and participating in local issues, events, and politics—are all good ways to become part of your new community.

After you've been in your new town for awhile, you'll see many opportunities to suggest, initiate, and lead new projects. You'll be a source of new ideas and fresh energy. You don't have to contend for volunteer of the year; do what you can. Whether you like to lead or prefer to work behind the scenes, whether you like high visibility or prefer to contribute in more private ways, your efforts will be valued. Every contribution will become part of the fabric of your town. Years later, you'll proudly smile at all of the strands you have woven.

If there is a single point to this chapter, it is this: The more successfully you settle into your new town, the sooner you will enjoy the benefits of life in a smaller community. Be as flexible and adaptable as you can when you settle in. Get involved. Contribute. Before long, you'll feel right at home. You will look back at your previous life and wonder why you didn't move to a small town years earlier. We predict you'll feel as we do:

We can't imagine being anywhere else. And we certainly can't imagine going back.

....

Moving to a small town is not instant gratification. It's a long-term commitment to getting involved.

—Cindy M.

Resource Appendix

This appendix is designed to help you research the information you need quickly. It is organized alphabetically by topic. Within each topic, you'll find a list of any books that we found particularly helpful, informal or unusual channels for getting information, and tips and suggestions. You'll also find commentary based on our own research experiences. Note that many of the general resources, such as government agencies, can refer you to local counterparts. Telephone numbers are apt to change frequently. If a number listed below is no longer in service, call Directory Assistance in the same area code for the new number.

Alternative Workstyles

These organizations can give you information and guidance on a variety of work arrangements, such as telecommuting, job sharing and working part time.

Association of Part-time Professionals
Falls Church, Virginia
(703) 734-7975

Catalyst
New York, New York
(212) 777-8900

New Ways to Work
San Francisco, California
(415) 995-9860

For people who are struggling to accommodate the demands of working and parenting, the following book contains descriptions of jobs that might help you achieve a better balance.

The Best Jobs in America for Parents Who Want Careers and Time for Children Too by Susan Bacon Dynerman and Lynn O'Rourke Hayes. Ballantine Books, 1992

(See *Small and Home Businesses* for more information.)

Arts and Culture

The most helpful contacts we found are the county Chambers of Commerce and Visitors Bureaus. State governments often have contacts as well for larger and state-funded organizations. See *State Information Agencies* listed below.

If the performing arts are a serious consideration for you, you might want to contact the following for additional information on the history of organizations, events, funding, and other aspects of performing arts in a particular area:

> Performing Arts Library
> John F. Kennedy Center
> Washington, DC 20566
> (202) 707-6245

Associations

A three-volume listing of all the associations in the U.S. you can imagine, available as a reference in most libraries, is:

> *Encyclopedia of Associations,* Gale Research, Inc., Detroit, 1993

Another source for extensive listings of associations throughout the U.S. is:

> American Society of Association Executives
> 1575 "I" Street NW
> Washington, DC 20005-1168
> (202) 626-2723

Business and Commerce

A useful national resource for all kinds of reference information and material about business and commerce in the U.S. is:

U.S. Department of Commerce
14th Street and Constitution Avenue NW
Washington, DC 20230
General information: (202) 482-2000

The Chamber of Commerce is often an excellent and willing source
of information and help. Contact the Washington office for general
information and a listing of state chapters. Check with the state chapters
for listings of local chapters.

Chamber of Commerce of the United States
1615 "H" Street NW
Washington, DC 20062
General Information: (202) 659-6000
Publications fulfillment: (301) 468-5128

Career Change

No matter what you do for a living, from gardening to geophysics, there
is an association, organization, or lobbying group somewhere that represents
you. It is worth your while to find it. Such associations acquire information about changing locations, promoting yourself in a new location,
getting hired in a different state, and the name of a local professional
organization you can contact. Frequently there will be one person
assigned the duty of promoting the expansion of the field. If you are
moving someplace where your profession is not already established, the
association may be willing to give you special assistance to relocate.

Bookstores and libraries offer scores of books on career change and
development. The following book has a lot to offer. Every year it is
revised and updated. A classic in its field, it takes the same approach to
finding the right job or career as *My Kind of Town* takes to finding the
right place to live. It offers practical information on job hunting, career
changing, profiling your ideal career based on your interests and skills,
upgrading your present job, and many other important topics.

What Color Is Your Parachute? by Richard Nelson Bolles
Ten Speed Press, (annual editions)

Census Data

The Bureau of the Census offers a wealth of information, more than most of us can even imagine. A complete listing of the products and services offered by the U.S. Bureau of the Census, such as pamphlets, books, slides, graphs, and maps, is available at some libraries, at the Federal Depository Library at the federal building in your area, or from the Government Printing Office (see *Government Information, Federal*):

> *Census Catalog and Guide*
> GPO stock number: 003-024-08752-9

To contact the Bureau of the Census directly:

> U.S. Bureau of the Census
> Public Information Office
> Room 2705, Federal Building #3
> Washington, DC 20233-8200
> Customer services: (301) 763-4100
> Public affairs: (301) 763-4040
> Fax: (301) 763-4794

The Bureau of the Census is also an excellent resource for statistical information about the U.S. Data are available on housing, schools, population, state and local governments, transportation, and many other topics. Call the customer services number above for a complete listing of department phone numbers.

For computer on-line services, contact CENDATA at (301) 763-2074. This service is available on CompuServe (see *On-Line Information*). It offers the most recent information for towns and counties.

The Climate

Statistics on average conditions in a region can be found in *Climates of the States*, listed below. In this book, climatic statistics are broken down by state and are based on averages of conditions from 1951 through 1980. It gives you the number of days above and below certain temperatures so you can calculate how many days you'll have those heaters or air conditioners running. If your library doesn't have it, ask about interlibrary loans.

Climates of the States
Gale Research, Inc., 1995

Local realtors are also an excellent source for the sizes of average heating and cooling bills for a given size house. Additional sources for climatic information are the U.S. Environmental Data Service, the U.S. Geological Survey, and the National Oceanographic and Atmospheric Administration.

Crime
For general crime-rate statistics broken down by region, the best resource is:

Uniform Crime Reporting Program
FBI / GRB
9th Street and Pennsylvania Avenue NW
Washington, DC 20535
(202) 324-5038

Each state has statistics available on crime rates, as well as on state and local police and fire funding. The agencies in charge of this information vary from state to state. Generally, it is the Department of Justice, the Department of Public Safety, or the State Police Department.

Demographics
There is a wide variety of demographic data that are generated by the Bureau of the Census. Information pertaining to a region's total population, age breakdowns, ethnic mix, and more can be found here:

Demographic Statistics
Bureau of the Census
Public Information Office
Room 2705, Federal Building #3
Washington, DC 20233-8200
(301) 763-4100

Directories of Resources and Information
The weighty reference book *Instant Information* contains names and

numbers of government agencies, corporations, trade associations, universities, think tanks, nonprofit agencies, and other sources of information. The book is organized alphabetically by state. There is an alphabetical listing of all agencies in the back. Though it may no longer be in print as you read this, many libraries still have copies of this useful book:

Instant Information by Joel Makower and Alan Green
Prentice Hall Press, 1987

Lesko's Info-Power is an extremely useful book, as big as a medium-sized city's phone directory. The front cover of our edition of this behemoth boasts, "Over 30,000 Free and Low Cost Sources of Information for Investors, Job Seekers, Teachers, Students, Artists, Travelers, Businesses Consumers, Homeowners, Techies, Communities, and MORE!" We believe it. It offers an invaluable starting point, listing numerous federal and state agencies, as well as associations and nonprofit agencies, that will lead you to the information you seek. The first eight pages, entitled "Information is Power," are worth the price of the book. They are an excellent guide to getting the information you want from any large bureaucracy, be it public or private.

Lesko's Info-Power by Matthew Lesko
Information USA, Inc., 1990

The Economy

The personality of a small town can be greatly influenced by the nature of and health of its economy, and towns only a few miles apart can have markedly different economies. Every state collects and maintains economic data. To find the state information, see *State Information Agencies* below. The appropriate state agency, in turn, will be able to provide the names of other regional, county, or municipal agencies with similar information.

In addition, there are several national resources of useful economic information:

Economic Statistics
Bureau of the Census
Public Information Office
Room 2705, Federal Building #3
Washington, DC 20233
(301) 763-4100

Public Information Office / BE-53
Bureau of Economic Analysis
Department of Commerce
Washington, DC 20230
(202) 606-9900

There is also a federal electronic on-line and fax service that allows you access to recent information from the Bureau of Economic Analysis, Bureau of the Census, Bureau of Labor Statistics, and other governmental entities:

National Trade Databank and Economic Bulletin Board
U.S. Department of Commerce
Office of Business Analysis & Economic Affairs
Washington, DC 20230
(202) 482-1986

See *On-Line Information* for more about electronic resources.

Education
To find out the test-score percentiles of a school district, contact:

Education Statistics
National Center for Education Statistics
Department of Education
1200 19th Street NW
Washington, DC 20208
(202) 219-1652

Each State Department of Education is also an excellent resource and should be able to provide you with: test-score percentiles by school; the state's and region's educational philosophies; the funds made available to schools per student and as a percentage of the state's total budget; and the funds available for special education programs, such as Head Start, Special Ed, and Talented and Gifted (TAG) student programs. Call the *State Information Agencies* (see below) for names of people to talk with about education statistics, philosophy, and issues in a specific region.

For information on the education level of a small town, the *County and City Data Books* (see *Government Information, Local and Regional* for ordering information) have statistics on the number of high school drop-outs, the number of college graduates, and other related data.

The Environment

It is not a bad idea to know something about the local environmental issues before you choose to live in a place. Here are some starting points.

The federal Environmental Protection Agency is the agency charged with oversight of the nation's environment. Like all federal agencies, it is very, very big. It has volumes of general and location-specific information. Persistence will pay off.

U.S. EPA
Public Information Center (3404)
401 M Street SW
Washington, DC 20460
(202) 260-7751

The EPA has many on-line databases, but it is probably more efficient to contact one of its regional libraries for specific information about an area. Regional libraries exist in Boston, New York, Edison, Philadelphia, Atlanta, Chicago, Dallas, Kansas City, Denver, San Francisco, and Seattle. For a comprehensive directory to the EPA's services, order *Access EPA* from the Government Printing Office, (202) 783-3238, GPO order number: 055-000-00437-4.

Another useful federal organization is the National Environmental Satellite, Data, and Information Service. It acts as a clearinghouse to identify existing private, federal, and state data about the environment, including all data and information acquired by NOAA's satellites. Contact:

NESDIS
2069 Federal Building #4
Washington, DC 20233
(301) 763-7190

The Council on Environmental Quality is an advisory council to the President of the U.S. on environmental issues. It publishes the annual *Environmental Quality Report* describing the environmental activities of governmental agencies and private organizations.

Council on Environmental Quality
722 Jackson Place NW
Washington, DC 20503
(202) 395-5750

It may be easier to pull specific information from private organizations than governmental. Many are more narrowly focused on a specific set of environmental problems. Local chapters can give you in-depth information about the areas you are considering. The following is just one of many organizations that provide environmental information to the public.

The Sierra Club is one of the nation's oldest and most active environmental organizations. Its focus is land use and other, related issues. It is built around a network of active local chapters. Regardless of how you feel about the Sierra Club's politics, as a source of regional environmental information the local chapters are probably unmatched.

The Sierra Club
730 Polk Street
San Francisco, CA 94109
(415) 776-2211

Franchises
For information on purchasing and running a franchise business, contact:

International Franchise Association
1350 New York Avenue NW
Washington, DC 20005
(202) 628-8000

(See *Small and Home Businesses* for more information.)

Government Information, Federal
The U.S. government is a gigantic bureaucracy. We came to think of it as a single cavernous room where thousands of people toil over thousands of desks forming neat lines that vanish into the distance. Each desk has a telephone. The good news is that at one of those thousands of desks is a person who has zealously devoted his or her entire career to studying the very information you seek. If you can reach that one right desk, you

will justify the person's entire life's work by granting him or her the honor of answering your question. And, to be honest, it is occasionally an exasperating-to-infuriating exercise to reach that single desk. To find the right desk, contact:

> Federal Information Center
> P.O. Box 600
> Cumberland, MD 21501-0600
> (301) 722-9000

For a listing of government information pamphlets and other materials, stop by the Federal Depository Library at the federal building in your area, or write:

> U.S. Government Printing Office
> P.O. Box 371954
> Pittsburgh, PA 15250

or call:
> (202) 512-1800

Another good resource, available at most libraries, is:

> *Guide to Popular U.S. Government Publications* by William G. Bailey
> Libraries Unlimited, Inc., 1993

Government Information, Local and Regional
This book, organized by cities and counties, contains statistical information on business, climate, crime, education, employment, health care, housing, income, population, and much more:

> *County and City Data Book 1994*
> U.S. Government Printing Office
> (202) 512-1800

A similar book, available at some libraries, is:

> *County and City Data Book: Statistics on States, Counties, Cities and Places in the United States*
> Gordon Press, 1991

Health Care

A lot has been written recently on the lack of specialists, especially obstetricians, in nonmetropolitan areas. If you are in the medical profession, the chances are that you will be a welcome addition to any small town. In fact, some small towns are aggressively recruiting medical professionals.

For statistics on hospital and doctor availability, refer to the *County and City Data Books* (see the listing immediately above). These resources also have statistics on the amount of health care funding allocated on local levels. The State Health Department (sometimes called the Department of Public Health) can also provide a variety of statistics and general information on health care availability, infectious diseases, hospital services, and other subjects.

Housing

See *Census Data* and *Government Information, Local and Regional,* above. The recent census provides cost-of-living and cost-of-housing data. It also provides much more specific information, such as the proportion of new and old housing in an area; the percentage of small versus large houses; and property tax rates.

Income

Per capita income statistics and projected income growth by area are available through the Census Bureau in the *Current Population Reports* (see *Census Data* above.)

Labor Statistics

For general employment, unemployment, and productivity statistics, contact:

Bureau of Labor Statistics
Department of Labor
441 G Street NW
Washington, DC 20212
Information: (202) 606-7828

State labor offices provide information on wages and employment by occupation, projections of industry growth and job growth by category, general economic information, and other statistics. Much of this information is broken down by county. Most states also have a Division of Corporations that provides detailed information on the state's private and public companies.

Manufacturing

Manufacturing productivity, diversity, and growth statistics are available through the Census Bureau (see *Census Data*) and in the *County and City Data Books* (see *Government Information, Local and Regional*).

Maps

Topographical maps provide a hefty amount of information. Unlike regular road maps, they show you the terrain. From a topo map you can see how many lakes, rivers, and reservoirs there are in an area. You can determine whether a town is in a valley, on a high mountainous ridge, or near a marsh. Hiking trails, recreation areas, fire roads, and major landmarks, such as airports and schools, are indicated.

To order topographical maps or other products for a specific region, contact the U.S. Geological Survey. Allow a few weeks for the information to reach you.

USGS Branch of Distribution
P.O. Box 25286 MS306, DFC
Denver, CO 80225
(303) 236-7477

One lesser-known service of the USGS is a series of very affordable aerial photographs of many areas of the country. These can be ordered from:

Earth Sciences Information Center
(303) 236-5829

Media

If you absolutely have to have access to a certain radio or cable or network TV station, there are several ways you can determine availability in small-town areas. For example, if you don't want to live without National Public Radio, contact the Public Broadcast station in the city closest to the small town you're considering and ask if they broadcast NPR. Then ask to speak with a broadcast engineer. Ask if the reception is good in the town you are considering. Most broadcast engineers are intimately familiar with their station's antennae, repeaters, and areas of strong (or not so strong) reception, and they tend to be somewhat more frank than the marketing personnel. When you visit the town, make sure you actually try to get NPR on your car radio. These same questions are valid for any radio station, cable television station, or network that matters to you.

A note about cable; it has come to small-town America in a big way. In some towns you have numerous media options, including commercial broadcast TV, cable TV, public radio broadcasting, and even community access stations. However, in other towns (like ours, because of surrounding mountains) you must pay for cable to receive any TV stations at all. The FCC is under pressure to increase regulation of cable TV stations. This could mean lower rates and better services in the future. Check the phone book for the small town you are considering and contact local cable stations for detailed information.

In the event that cable has not made it to a town you are considering, you may wish to explore the option of a satellite dish. Check the local phone book for the vendors of satellite dishes and related equipment.

For statistics on how many radio, TV, and cable stations are available in a town, check your library for this three-volume reference set:

Gale Directory of Publications and Broadcast Media
(Formerly *Ayer Directory of Publications*)
Gale Research, Inc., (annual)

The most useful medium of all in any small town to which you might move is the local newspaper. We strongly recommend that you subscribe, to learn a lot about the intangibles—the general tenor and tone of the town. Often the Chamber of Commerce or Visitors Bureau will send you a free copy of the local paper as a courtesy.

Newsletters

In March 1994, Lisa Agnowski Rogak published the first issue of her bimonthly newsletter "*STICKS . . . for people who are serious about moving to the country.*" She is a transplant from Brooklyn, New York, to rural New England. Articles include "Should You Lose Your New York Accent?", "Town Profile: Woodstock Vermont," and "What to Look For When You're Buying a Farm." *STICKS* approaches the issue of moving out of the city from an East Coast perspective, though there is much here for westerners as well.

STICKS
Moose Mountain Press
RR 1, Box 1234
Grafton, NH 03240

Another newsletter that focuses on helping people make the transition from cities to America's small towns and rural areas is *Greener Pastures*. The Greener Pastures Institute offers classes as well.

Greener Pastures
P.O. Box 2190
Henderson, NY 89009

On-Line Information

An increasing amount of information is available electronically. You can access a multitude of databases from your local library or your personal computer. If you want to conduct research from your personal computer, you will need a modem.

Most consumer on-line service companies offer easy access to information on specific topics, such as finance, news, travel, education, or computer usage. A few of them enable you to hook up to the databases of other services, libraries, or government agencies via the Internet. You can also use on-line services to "talk" to people about topics of mutual interest. For example, if you're interested in learning more about the advantages and disadvantages of small-town lifestyles, you might participate in or start a discussion on this topic with other computer users all over the U.S.

The following are some of the better known, general consumer on-line information services. Contact them directly for details on their services and costs.

America Online	(800) 827-6364
CompuServe	(800) 848-8990
Delphi	(800) 544-4005
Dow Jones News/Retrieval	(800) 522-3567

Prodigy   (800) 776-0836

The Well   (415) 332-4335

Libraries and government agencies are using a multitude of electronic databases these days. If you are new to these services, someone at your local public or university library can give you an overview of how they work.

Politics

The political scene in the communities you are researching can be looked into by contacting these groups locally. Look in the local phone book for:

The League of Women Voters
The Republican Party
The Democratic Party
American Association of University Women

If you are interested in more specific information about the political character of a community, there are several resources. For statistics on the voter turnout of a town or a region, contact:

Elections Research Center
(301) 654-3540

For a listing of political, cultural, social, religious, and environmental organizations in a small town, contact the town's Visitors Bureau, the Chamber of Commerce, or the mayor's office.

To learn about the daily down and dirty, the town's newspaper is often an excellent source. With it you can gauge how truly active the community is on a day-to-day level. Small-town reporters and editors are usually much more accessible than their urban cousins. If you have a specific question and can't find the answer elsewhere, it's a good bet that a local editor or reporter will know.

Population

The Bureau of the Census provides extensive statistics on current population density and projected population growth. (See *Census Data*.)

Professional and Trade Associations
See *Associations.*

Recreation
Call the state Information Agency in the areas you are researching. Request a name and number of someone to talk to in the Office of Tourism. Most states will send you a brochure highlighting the state's recreational facilities free of charge.

Another good contact is the National Park Service. *The National Parks: Index* describes the facilities made available through the national park system. To order, contact:

Superintendent of Documents
Government Printing Office
P.O. Box 371954
Pittsburgh, PA 15250
(202) 512-1800

The *Recreation Guide to BLM Public Lands* provides information on Bureau of Land Management lands designated as recreational areas. Contact:

Publication Information
U.S. Department of the Interior
Bureau of Land Management
1849 "C" Street NW
Washington, DC 20240
(202) 208-5717

Religion
If you practice a religion, a small-town church, synagogue, or parish of your denomination can be an excellent source of information about a community. Your current place of worship will probably have a national directory of the churches, synagogues, or parishes of your religion. It is an excellent way to make initial contacts in the small towns you are contemplating.

Restaurants

The *County and City Data Books,* listed under *Government Information, Local and Regional,* offers statistics on the number of eating and drinking establishments in a particular area. Chambers of Commerce and Visitors Bureaus are also excellent resources; once you have narrowed your areas of choice, the local phone books will offer more detailed and specific information.

Retail Sales

The Census Bureau determines retail sales statistics by calculating a town's total retail revenue divided by the number of local residents, including children. This information is often an indicator of the town's overall economic health. (See *Census Data.*)

Also, check out the statistics in the *County Business Patterns* pamphlet. This subscription resource lists the number of food outlets, department stores, clothing and shoe stores, and other retail outlets in a particular area. It is available at university business libraries, federal libraries, or for $290 a year from:

U.S. Government Printing Office
P.O. Box 371954
Pittsburgh, PA 15250
(202) 512-1800

Shopping

If you were born to shop and want to make sure the small town you choose offers more than hardware stores and farm supplies, you will want to check out the statistics in the County Business Patterns listed directly above. This resource lists the number of food outlets, department stores, clothing and shoe stores, and other retail outlets in a particular area.

Singles Activities

The phone book is a good resource for finding out about singles' clubs, the local night life, and other activities; for whatever you are specifically interested in, a singles' groups may exist or be worth organizing. A number of Sierra Club chapters sponsor singles' outings, for example.

Small and Home Businesses

There are many sources of information on how to start and run a small or home business, how to buy a franchise, and what the best business opportunities are for the coming decade. They range from detailed tax and bookkeeping workbooks to "you-can-do-it!" pep pamphlets. Below are several excellent resources. Check in the business section of your local library and bookstores to find the books that best meet your needs.

Some of the best books we've come across on starting and running a home business are by Sarah and Paul Edwards. They offer nuts and bolts advice, insights on business trends for the 1990s, and lots of useful tips. We highly recommend:

Working from Home: Everything You Need to Know about Living and Working Under the Same Roof by Paul and Sarah Edwards, Putnam Publishing Group, 1994

and also

The Best Home Businesses for the 90s by Paul and Sarah Edwards, Jeremy P. Tarcher, Inc., 1991

Several other books you might want to check out (the last one with specific information about mail-order and franchise businesses) are:

Small-Time Operator: How to Start Your Own Small Business, Keep Your Books, Pay Your Taxes, and Stay out of Trouble! by Bernard Kamoroff, C.P.A., Bell Springs Publishing, 1993

Starting on a Shoestring: Build a Business without a Bankroll by Arnold S. Goldstein, Ph.D., John Wiley and Sons, 1991

How to Run a Small Business by J.K. Lasser Tax Institute, McGraw-Hill, 1993

Of the federal agencies, the best known is the Small Business Administration. For information on how to start and run a small business, financing resources, the addresses and numbers of regional SBA offices, and a listing of agency publications, call this toll-free hotline:

1 (800) U ASK SBA (827-5722)

At the state level, labor offices can provide you with information on local salary ranges, the number of similar businesses in an area, the availability of skilled workers in an area, the state's equal opportunity requirements, and more.

There is also a newsletter, *Relocatable Business,* for people interested in purchasing a business that is not bound by geographic limitations. It advertises that the businesses it lists are ones you can "buy and move and operate anywhere in the country without losing customers." For more information, contact:

Business Listing Services, Inc.
P.O. Box 1248
Highland Park, IL 60035
(800) 927-1310

Sports

Generally, sports are a big deal in the local schools of small towns. The Visitors Bureau and Chamber of Commerce can offer lots of information on sports activities and funding at the K-12, higher-education, and professional levels.

State and Local Funding

How much money does a state or county allocate for recreation facilities, schools, or road improvements? This information can be found through the Census Bureau in its *Census of Governments: Compendium of Government Finances.* (See *Census Data* for the latest GPO ordering information.)

State Information Agencies

Every state has some type of a general information agency, which you can find by calling directory assistance in the state capitol. These agencies exist solely to help you find the information you seek. Most have brochures highlighting their state's strong points and providing basic statistical information and will send them to you free of charge or for a nominal fee. The state information agencies can also direct you to other departments to help you gather specific information about that particular state's tax structure, recreational facilities, or other concern.

Statistics
See *Census Data*.

Taxes
State taxpayer departments are called different names in different states, such as the Franchise Tax Board or Department of Revenue. Call *State Information Agencies* (see above) for referrals to the state agencies that can provide you with information about states' income, property, and sales tax rates.

Property tax rates can also be learned from the Bureau of the Census and the *County and City Data Books* (see *Census Data* and *Government Information, Local and Regional*).

Telecommunications
To determine the level of telecommunications sophistication in a region or town, write or call the telephone company in that area. Ask what the switching capability is at this time, and what's planned for the future. If you have specific needs, such as for high-speed data transmission, ask if the company can accommodate your needs. Generally, the business side (as opposed to home service) of the phone company is better educated about special technology needs.

Transportation
A local map is often the best resource for determining road, railroad, and airport availability. Good maps are available from Rand-McNally, the American Automobile Association, and local Visitors Bureaus. Also see *Maps*.

Each state has a department of transportation that can provide you with current and future public transportation data. In addition, many rural counties offer some form of public transportation, from full bus service to door-to-door van services for nondrivers needing transportation to stores, medical facilities, and so on. To find out about local and regional public transportation, call the county transportation district in the area you are investigating.

Urban Proximity

If you are seeking a small town that isn't hours away from the closest city or, on the other hand, you want to make sure a small town is far enough away from the city, check a good atlas or state maps. Make sure the map is fairly recent! Some areas have grown so fast in the past few years that what was recently a small town miles away may now be a seamless adjunct to urban sprawl.

Blank
Worksheets

The Quality-of-Life Worksheet

Before you start this Worksheet, repeat Rule 6 out loud:
Change your mind whenever you need to.

Step 5   One attractive quality-of-life characteristic of my kind of town is:

_____

_____

Step 6   Describe what this quality-of-life characteristic *really* means:

_____

_____

_____

_____

_____

Step 7   Prioritize this quality-of-life characteristic:

A must-have   _____

Very desirable   _____

A good idea   _____

Might be nice   _____

Step 8   Describe research resources for this quality-of-life characteristic:

_____

_____

_____

_____

_____

[photocopy this page]

The Search Worksheet Part A

Patience + persistence = good research.

Step 11 Name the likely towns.

Step 9 List the employment must-haves, the most geographically limiting first.

1 _____

2 _____

3 _____

4 _____

5 _____

Step 12 Investigate and evaluate each town.

Step 9 List quality-of-life must-haves, the most geographically limiting first.

1 _____

2 _____

3 _____

4 _____

5 _____

Step 10 On a map of the entire area you are considering, outline regions that do not meet your must-haves and mark them out of the running. Draw another color border around those that do. Apply as many must-haves and other characteristics as necessary to pinpoint a researchable number of likely towns.

[photocopy this page]

The Search Worksheet Part B

Step 11   Name the likely towns.

Step 9   List the other attractive characteristics, in order of importance.

Step 12   Evaluate each town.

[photocopy this page]

The Shortlist Worksheet

This worksheet is dedicated to the town of: _____

Before you start this Worksheet, repeat Rule 3 out loud:
Feelings are as important as facts.

Step 13   List the benefits of this town:

_____

_____

_____

_____

_____

_____

Step 14   List the drawbacks of this town:

_____

_____

_____

_____

_____

Step 15   List any remaining questions about this town:

_____

_____

_____

_____

_____

_____

[photocopy this page]

Selected
Bibliography

Barlett, Donald L., and James B. Steele. *America: What Went Wrong?*
Andrews and McMeel, 1992

Bolles, Richard Nelson. *What Color Is Your Parachute?* Ten Speed Press,
(Annual editions)

Dominguez, Joe, and Vicki Robin. *Your Money or Your Life: Transforming
Your Relationship with Money and Achieving Financial Independence.*
Viking Penguin, 1992

Fisher, Roger, and William Ury. *Getting to Yes: Negotiating Agreement
Without Giving In (2nd edition).* Penguin Books, 1991

Heenan, David A. *The New Corporate Frontier: The Big Move to Small
Town U.S.A.* McGraw Hill, 1991

Hiss, Tony. *The Experience of Place: A New Way of Looking at and
Dealing with Our Radically Changing Cities and Countryside.* Vintage
Books, 1990

Lesko, Matthew. *Lesko's Info Power.* Information USA, 1990

McLuhan, Marshall, and Quentin Fiore. *The Medium Is the Message.*
Touchstone, 1967

McLuhan, Marshall, and Bruce R. Powers. *The Global Village:
Transformations in World Life and Media in the 21st Century.* Oxford
University Press, 1989

Popcorn, Faith. *The Popcorn Report.* Doubleday, 1991

Rebeck, George. "Saving America's Small Towns" *The Utne Reader,* Nov. / Dec. 1991

Santayana, George. *Little Essays.* Edited by Logan Pearsall Smith. Charles Scribner's Sons, 1920

Schumacher, E. F. *Small Is Beautiful: Economics as if People Mattered.* Harper & Row, 1973

Shaffer, Carolyn R., and Kristin Anundsen. *Creating Community Anywhere: Finding Support and Connection in a Fragmented World.* Jeremy P. Tarcher / Perigee, 1993

Toffler, Alvin. *The Third Wave.* Bantam Books, 1980

Welles, Edward O. *Virtual Realities. Inc. Magazine,* August 1993

Williams, Tennessee. *Camino Real.* New Directions, 1970

Index